HOW TO GET THE BEST ADVERTISING FROM YOUR AGENCY

HOW TO GET THE BEST ADVERTISING FROM YOUR AGENCY

HOW IT WORKS, HOW TO WORK WITH IT... A MANAGEMENT PRIMER FOR ADVERTISERS.

SECOND EDITION

NANCY L. SALZ

DOW JONES-IRWIN
Homewood, Illinois 60430

This publication is designed to provide accurate and authoritative information in regard to the subject matter covered. It is sold with the understanding that neither the author nor the publisher is engaged in rendering legal, accounting, or other professional service. If legal advice or other expert assistance is required, the services of a competent professional person should be sought.

From a Declaration of Principles jointly adopted by a Committee of the American Bar Association and a Committee of Publishers.

Acquisitions editor: Susan Glinert Stevens, Ph.D.
Project editor: Joan A. Hopkins
Production manager: Bette Ittersagen
Compositor: Caliber Design Planning, Inc.
Typeface: 11/13 Century Schoolbook
Printer: Arcata Graphics/Kingsport

Library of Congress Cataloging-in-Publication Data
Salz, Nancy L.
How to get the best advertising from your agency.

Includes index.
1. Advertising agencies. 2. Advertising.
I. Title.
HF6178.S24   1988   659.1'068   87-73242
ISBN 1-55623-107-5

Printed in the United States of America
2 3 4 5 6 7 8 9 0 K 5 4 3 2 1 0 9 8

For Irving M. Clyne

Foreword

The client-agency relationship is one of the most complex in business—and one of the most important.

It is complex because both sides are working on different parts of a single chore. And as the work is passed back and forth—first from client to agency after product, pricing, and market-position decisions are made, then back from agency to client after communication decisions and executions are done— the facts and rationale from each side must be understood and accepted by the other if the total marketing thrust is to be cohesive and forceful.

That understanding is forever complicated because it is rooted partly in facts, and in larger part in personal judgment. Science and art share the stage and fight for the spotlight.

There is eternal wisdom in Raymond Rubicam's remark that "a good advertising man is a good explainer."

In spite of, or because of, such problems, the client-agency relationship is always fantastic—either good or bad. It is never so-so, or average.

How to achieve a healthy relationship is what this book is about. It tackles its complex mission by first explaining all the things an agency does and how, and then explaining the client's role in instructing, assisting, interpreting, encouraging, and evaluating the agency's work.

Most agency arrangements stumble over misunderstandings of what is expected of the agency by the client or vice versa. The great contribution of this book is that it identifies and explains exactly what goes on in all these areas where misunderstandings may be generated.

It is, indeed, a long list. In fact, as you read, if you feel that the list is practically endless, you are beginning to get the right idea.

Only by learning what all the chores are and how to handle them can you become a "great client." That is a very worthy ambition and a somewhat rare achievement.

Henry Schachte
Weston, Connecticut

Contents

Preface to the second edition

Here are some startling facts that have been discovered since the first edition of this book was published.

The top 100 advertising agencies report that they are able to do their best work for only 59 percent of their major clients. That means only about one out of two advertisers is getting the best possible advertising for his money.

Not surprisingly, the top 200 advertisers report that they are barely satisfied with the advertising they are getting from their agencies—rating it only 7.1 on a 1 to 10 scale.

However, these same advertisers predict that, if they got their agencies' best advertising all the time they would see a *24 percent increase in sales and a 23 percent increase in profits*.

We can draw one crucial conclusion from these facts: There is a huge opportunity for you to work more productively with your agency, get better advertising, and increase your sales and profits.

This book, although I have tried to make it fast paced and interesting to read, is about a very serious subject, your bottom line. The above statistics, from the 1987 Salz Survey of Advertiser-Agency Relations (see Appendix), show just how vital your management skills are in working with your agency. Advertisers who have them get better work than those who don't. It's just that simple.

Until the original edition of this book appeared, many advertisers were perplexed about how to work with their agencies. Consequently, they not only didn't get the quality of advertising they could have but also they were often quite uncomfortable giving direction to their agency and critiquing their agency's work.

The most gratifying part of my work, both writing this book and presenting seminars, has been seeing "light bulbs go on," seeing people understand that, with a little knowledge, working with an agency isn't so perplexing after all. Not only are many readers and those who attend our seminars indeed getting the best advertising from their agencies, they're having a lot more fun and satisfaction in the process.

So many people have helped, and I would like to take this opportunity to thank them: First, Gertrude R. Crain; next, Harry Paster and Marilyn Bockman of the American Association of Advertising Agencies; those who contributed their wisdom to this edition—Ray Abrahamsen, Kathleen Cantwell, Charles G. Francis, Debra Goldstein, Mary Kay Haben, Shiela Hopkins, Edward C. MacEwen, Ann Marcato, F. Kent Mitchel, Robert K. Powell, Thomas Raikakos, Allen Rosenshine, Brian Ruder, Stephen W. Rutledge, Lee C. Tashjian, Jr., Connie Sartain, Pete Tyrrell, Sy Waldman, Thomas Watson, Joel D. Weiner, and Robert E. Williams—plus all those mentioned in the original preface.

I would also like to thank my always helpful and enthusiastic new editor, Dr. Susan Glinert.

Preface

How to Get the Best Advertising from Your Agency is not another book about solving advertising problems or a text on how to create advertising. It is a guide for junior advertisers, entrepreneurs, and students to the management of a special group of people: the copywriters, art directors, and members of an agency's account management group who create the advertising for your product or service. Because agency people are the "machinery" that produce the advertising product, how you manage them will in large part determine the quality of the advertising they create for you.

I know from personal experience. In my 20 years in the advertising business—in creative as well as account management—I have had clients who managed the agency well and with whom I wanted to work, and I have had clients with whom it was merely my job to work. For the former, I devoted more time and enthusiasm than I should have. For the latter, well, I quickly completed their assignments so that I could work for the former. I have observed similar behavior in my colleagues over the years, and many of the agency people interviewed for this book have confirmed it.

Until the publication of *How to Get the Best Advertising from Your Agency* there has been little information available to teach young advertising managers, product managers, entrepreneurs, and students how to manage an advertising agency and obtain the best efforts of its people. Senior advertisers have discussed managerial problems with senior agency management, but too few companies formally train the lower-level people who must form a relationship with agency people and work with them daily.

This book will teach you how to get the best advertising from your agency first by helping you understand the organization and people involved in the advertising creative process. In the first three chapters, I have explained why outstanding advertising is so important to you, your agency management, account management, and creative people. I have then set forth the relationship that produces the best advertising and explained how to establish and maintain that relationship throughout the creative development process. Finally, I have included some case histories of problems you may encounter.

There are several facts of which you should be aware before you start reading the text. First, I have assumed you know your advertising ABC's—that you've studied marketing and/or advertising. Second, I have focused on the creation of advertising and refer to media and marketing research only in their relationship to advertising creation. Media and marketing research are large, important areas that should be studied in far more depth than the information presented here. Third, I have chosen to exclude the separate field of direct response advertising. Direct response is so specialized, it is usually handled by direct response agencies. Many principles in this book are applicable to direct response; however, if you are using that medium, you should consult additional sources of information. Fourth, although the government has regulated advertising for many years, the specific regulations can vary by the political party in power. Therefore, you should consult an attorney in addition to this book to determine whether your advertising meets current regulations. Fifth, you should be aware that the opinions expressed by those people interviewed here reflect their personal viewpoints and not necessarily those of the companies for which they work. Sixth, titles reflect those at the time each person was interviewed and are not necessarily current. Last, because of the large number of women in marketing and advertising, the personal pronouns *he* and *she* are used interchangeably.

There are many people I want to thank for their help in writing this book. At the top of the list is Loretta McCarthy, who inspired the idea. Next, Sam Thurm, Tracy Kelly, and Peter Rosow, who read the material and offered thorough and most helpful criticism. Pam Adler, Susan Hudson, Jennifer Hudson, and Loretta McCarthy cheerfully endured my endless typing at our Sag Harbor summer house in 1982. Andrew Thurm helped organize my questionnaire and taught me how to conduct an interview. Mary Swartz and Tish O'Connor provided important encouragement when this book was at the proposal stage. Roberta Brenner and Jerry Hirsch introduced me to many of the people I interviewed. Herb Ahlgren, Tony Lunt, and Rosemary Collins of the Association of National Advertisers helped enormously with my preliminary research. Debra Goldstein contributed her knowledge of the regulatory process. Elaine Keeve and Ralph Papaleo contributed the details of broadcast and print production, respectively. Pat Tyler typed the manuscript during her entire Thanksgiving holiday, stopping only for a few bites of turkey. Elaine Potwardoski and Suzanne Gabriel helped with administrative work. And, of course, I thank my editor, Saul B. Cohen, for his initial interest, his personal support, and his invaluable advice.

Finally, I thank all the men and women I interviewed, those named below and those who, for personal reasons, wish to remain anonymous: Jeff Atlas, Tamar Bernbaum, Franchellie Cadwell, Frances Caldwell, Herman Davis, John Deford, Ellen Elias, Victor Elkind, Malcolm End, Claudia Garbin, Susan Hudson, J. Leonard Hultgren, Jane Steele Kaufman, Tracy Kelly, Abby Kohnstamm, Ronald Leong, Bob Neuman, Richard Rosenbloom, Bernard Rosner, Mary Seggerman, and Tim Tully.

HOW TO GET THE BEST ADVERTISING FROM YOUR AGENCY

chapter 1

The real power
behind great advertising

If you learn only one thing from reading this book, let it be this: You, the advertiser, are the person who ultimately creates great advertising.

Great advertising doesn't begin when a copywriter rolls blank paper into his typewriter or when an art director sketches a rough layout. It doesn't even begin when you call in the agency to brief them on your product or service. It begins with *you* and your vision of great advertising, your commitment to it, and your personal ability to create the relationship with agency people that nurtures great advertising.

Some advertisers get great advertising. Some get merely adequate work, even from the best agencies. In a speech before the Association of National Advertisers (ANA), William Claggett, vice president and director of Advertising and Marketing Services of the Ralston Purina Company, made that observation. He questioned, "Why is it that one company can consistently get better advertising than another company even when they both use the same advertising agency resource? Or, to carry the question a step further, why is it that two different product groups within the same company can get such different results from the same agency—and very often from the same creative team?"[1]

Often the answer is simply that some advertisers are better at managing their agency than others. They understand their agency, their agency people, and the advertising development process, and they have the skills to turn their understanding into superior work.

This book will give you first that understanding and then those skills so that you become an advertiser who gets the best advertising from your agency.

WHY IS ADVERTISING IMPORTANT?

The advertising business is not always a respected profession in this country. Even agency people acknowledge that fact. Jock Elliott, former chairman of Ogilvy & Mather International, often quotes the old saw: "Don't tell my mother I work in advertising; she thinks I play piano in a whorehouse."

As a consumer or college student, it's easy to share that poor impression of advertising. At its worst, advertising allegedly brainwashes innocent people into spending money they can't afford on goods and services they don't really need. At its best, advertising is informative and a major contributing factor to high-quality, reasonably priced goods and services.

As a marketer, you will quickly recognize and respect the power of this important marketing tool. Simply stated, advertising is the primary means of creating awareness for your product or service and persuading consumers to buy it. That's why an extraordinary amount of money is allocated to advertising by major companies every year.

- An estimated $109.8 billion was spent on advertising in 1987 and $102.1 billion in 1986.[2]
- In many companies advertising is the single largest expenditure—even higher than the total cost of goods.

The amount of money spent on advertising focuses on only one measurement of advertising's importance: the media expenditures. To fully appreciate the influence of advertising on business success, you must also consider the thousands of marketers and agency people who work to create the most effective advertising on which the media budget is spent. The effectiveness of advertising is determined by both the amount of money behind it and the effectiveness of the message.

WHAT IS GREAT ADVERTISING?

Advertising has three major objectives:

1. To create awareness—of a product, service, or, in the case of advocacy advertising, an issue.
2. To instill a positive attitude—toward the product, service, or point of view on an issue.

3. To persuade consumers—to purchase the product or service or to share the point of view.

Advertising that accomplishes these objectives is effective advertising, but the effectiveness of advertising can vary widely. In a study commissioned by the ANA, the management consulting firm of Booz • Allen & Hamilton observed, "In advertising, the selling power of a great idea can exceed that of an ordinary idea by a multiple of 10—or even more between extremes—even though the budgets supporting the two are identical."[3]

Good advertising, therefore, is effective advertising, advertising that achieves the objectives of creating awareness, instilling a positive attitude, and persuading consumers. *Better* advertising is more effective. However, for advertising to be the *best,* to be *great* advertising, it must inspire another element— *pride of association* because of both its effectiveness and the special creative way that effectiveness is achieved.

Think about that for a moment. Advertising is highly visible. It appears in the public media. Therefore, it not only creates awareness of and an attitude toward the product or service being advertised, it also creates an awareness of an attitude toward all the people who created and approved it. That includes *you.* And if your associates and management are going to see your work, you want to be proud of what they see.

ADVERTISING AND YOUR CAREER

In order for you to envision great advertising and become committed to it, you must first recognize how important it can be to you and your career. In any business organization, your identity is established by your contributions. "Who's Jane Smith? Jane Smith's the person who launched Superwhite Detergent." *The person who*—that's who *you* become. And the bigger and more visible the success that completes the sentence, the further it can carry you professionally.

Although advertising is by no means the only factor in professional success, it is of critical importance because it determines your personal contributions in two ways: It helps build sales and often is singly responsible for a business success, and it is highly visible. The business-building ability and visibility of advertising make this marketing tool important to you at every stage of your career.

- The product manager wants great advertising primarily to build sales, and also to create visibility for her brand with company management and to create visibility for her.
- The president of a small company wants outstanding advertising to build sales, to establish a favorable image for his company among service establishments within his community, such as banks, and to build his stature among competitors and even friends.
- Top management is concerned not only about sales effectiveness, but also about the image the advertising is creating: What does the advertising say about my company to our stockholders, the government, the business community? What does it say about me as a leader?

You may have the most advanced product or service to offer the world; you may have mastered the most sophisticated management techniques; you may have an education from the best business school; but if you don't have outstanding advertising to accompany them, you're in trouble. As a vice president and general manager of a major advertiser points out, "If you have a good, well-priced product and a good advertising campaign, you can kind of go to sleep and get rich. If you don't have both of those, you can manage your little fanny off from now till Christmas and you're never going to get rich."

"Fine," you may now think. "I'm convinced. I need great advertising. Tell me where to get it, and I'll go get some." If only it were that easy! You can't order up great advertising the way you can ask your research and development department for a new flavor cake mix or manufacturing for a new color toothbrush to expand your market. In most cases, you have to seek the expertise of an organization outside your company with its own structure, politics, and personality, and develop a continuing relationship with people over whom you have little direct authority, to help them create great advertising. Thus, working with an advertising agency is different from working with any other organization you'll encounter in your business career.

YOUR SOURCE OF GREAT ADVERTISING: THE ADVERTISING AGENCY

Virtually every top national advertiser has chosen to delegate the advertising function to an organization outside its own company: the advertising agency. Outside agencies usually create better advertising than in-house advertising departments. There are three major reasons why.

- Advertising is a product. Its primary means of production is people. As in any manufacturing operation, the production of advertising requires its own organization, priorities, and skills.
- Advertising is dependent on creativity—the development of ideas. People are most creative in an environment where creativity is the most important priority, where every resource is allocated toward the production of ideas. In a company that must have other priorities, such as manufacturing or the purchase of raw materials, creativity can be crushed—and creativity and advertising ideas are fragile.
- The solution to an advertising problem requires objectivity and a distance from the advertising problem as seen from the advertiser's perspective. Advertising is the communications link between the product and its consumers, and the agency must be able to bring *both* perspectives to the advertising. Advertisers, because their primary function is to produce a product or service at as large a profit as possible, are often too close to the product to see it from the consumer's perspective. (Objectivity is difficult when you're paying the bills!)

WORKING WITH AN AGENCY: THE CHALLENGES

You, as a product manager or president of a small business, must face a unique set of challenges when working with your agency; many of them are due to delegating the advertising function outside your company.

You must develop a continuing working relationship. The agency isn't hired on a project-by-project basis, as a packaging design firm might be. Rather, the agency is a group of people, chosen by you or your management on the basis of their manner of working, their personalities, as well as the advertising product they produce. The relationship is somewhat like a marriage, "for better or for worse," but if the worse tends to dominate, the relationship can be dissolved.

An agency is hired as a continuing business partner because, to create great advertising, the agency must be intimately involved in your business. Contrary to popular belief, major companies do not change agencies often. Corporations such as Procter & Gamble, General Foods, and Lever Brothers have been working with most of their agencies for 20 years or more.

You and your company must compete with other agency clients for the talent, time, and dedication of agency people. Not all clients are treated equally. One reason is that some clients are not as good at managing their agencies as others. They don't have the skills; they don't set high standards; they don't communicate well with their agencies. Another reason is agency profits. According to a senior advertiser executive: "My belief is that service organizations can't possibly afford, especially these days, to service clients as well as clients ought to be serviced, and I believe they make their profit on the difference between the maximum service that is theoretically required by all of their clients and the level of service they provide. It is unlikely that every client gets the same level of service. Some get overserviced. Some get serviced appropriately and some get badly underserviced."

If you are a product manager, you have a great deal of responsibility for the work of the agency, but very little authority over it. Any person below the level of president, director of marketing, or advertising manager has his role in relationship to the agency and the services provided by the agency predetermined for him.

As an advertising or product manager, you are responsible for the quality of the advertising created by the agency, yet you do not have the authority to approve work for production and airing. Your authority is limited to allowing or refusing permission for the agency to present their work to your management. Although the agency will be reluctant to use it, they usually have the option to go over your head and present copy in which they have strong belief. In sum, you have the authority to say "no" but not "yes."

In most cases, you are expected to work with a specific job level and a specific person at the agency. Agency account groups are usually structured to mirror the structure of the advertiser organization so that people at the same level of responsibility and expertise work together. Assistant product managers work with assistant account executives, and presidents work with presidents. It is, of course, at the highest level that the overall nature of the relationship between advertiser and agency is set, usually in the form of a contract.

The formal contract that exists between your organization and the agency specifies the services the agency is to provide, timing, means of compensation, ownership of material produced by the agency, and the basis upon which the contract can be terminated. All of this means that if you want services from the agency that are not covered in the contract, you probably will not obtain those services without an additional cost.

To summarize the special, indeed difficult, challenges facing an advertising manager, product manager, or president of a small business in working with an agency—you are the primary coordinator of the advertising produced by your agency, yet you must compete with other agency clients for services and work with people you have not selected in a continuing relationship that you cannot, except in extreme circumstances, terminate.

If you have little authority over the agency and little control over their work, how on earth do you get the agency to produce great advertising for you? You have to make them *want* to—by creating the right chemistry.

THE IMPORTANCE OF THE RIGHT CHEMISTRY

There isn't one bit of knowledge you have about marketing, strategies, analysis, developing options, or even the basics about what makes good advertising that is nearly as important as your personal ability to create the relationship in which creativity can thrive—in other words, creating the right chemistry.

To quote Marvin Bower of McKinsey & Company, "I suspect that few executives have a full appreciation of how importantly their decisions, actions, and attitudes affect the performance and morale of agency people. Any good professional is sensitive to the needs and wishes of his client, no matter how secure a position his firm provides him for differing with his client.

"The sophisticated and considerate advertiser executive will take advantage of this basic fact to get more from his agency. Every advertiser is in competition with other agency clients for the interest, effort, and dedication of agency personnel—and in this competition it is often the little things that count."[4]

You may be finding these comments difficult to accept. All through school and through many aspects of your career, you are judged on your ability to develop options, analyze them, and arrive at supportable conclusions, but advertising cannot be subject to the same analytical process. Advertising is part art and part science—created by people to motivate people. If it included only the facts about your product and the marketplace, it would read and sound like a marketing plan. It is the "art" part, the creative aspect, that makes advertising alive so that consumers can feel it and react to it.

Because advertising includes feelings, it is sensitive to the emotions of all the people involved in its creation and their relationship to each other. In fact, advertising is probably the business tool most sensitive to the people involved with it. According to Booz • Allen & Hamilton, "The relative effectiveness among product managers in leading others and getting action stems from their personal capabilities, not from their positions as such. . . . product managers who have established themselves as individuals . . . who help others get their jobs done—who are repeatedly connected with good results—soon find they have tacit authority every bit as useful as the real article. The product manager—or any other person in the marketing-advertising agency collaboration—who cannot get results through others he depends on, must be suspect as a suitable individual for his job.[5] Emphasis is on their capabilities and chemistry of and between personnel in advertiser and agency."[6]

Like it or not, you must realize that agency people will simply work harder and with more enthusiasm and dedication for advertisers whom they respect and like, and from whom they feel respect and trust. You have to become what agency people characterize as a good client. It makes all the difference, as the following quotes demonstrate. (The quotes are anonymous for obvious reasons.)

> By the time I left the agency, I was vice president, management supervisor on one of their most important accounts. Some of my clients I really broke my back for and others I didn't. In thinking about it, it became fairly clear to me that some clients were appropriately demanding, appropriately appreciative of the work, appropriately motivating and inspiring, and those were the ones I liked to work with. The ones that weren't any or all of those things got less of my time and less of the agency's time.
>
> *A former management supervisor*

> It took a few months, but that product manager managed to get herself literally despised by everyone at the agency. Her dictatorial attitude, lack of respect for the agency, and lack of advertising knowledge, plus her insistence that her exact words be used in all the advertising, led to creative people giving less than the minimum amount of time to her account, a boycott of senior people attending meetings with her . . . and ultimately rotten advertising, which is just what a rotten client deserves.
>
> *An agency account supervisor*

> We were treated by the bad clients basically like someone who would sell them printing. And when you don't feel respected and trusted, it's very hard to respond aggressively, intelligently, and enthusiastically.
>
> *A former management supervisor*

If he's not responding and it's very plain that there's a big philosophical difference or whatever and you have no respect for the guy or you just can't get around him, you're just not going to want to knock yourself out. You lose enthusiasm. On the other hand, if you get a client whom you respect, I think you develop a really good relationship and you enjoy working with him. He's getting more out of you.

A creative director

Work doesn't differ from the good clients to the bad clients. What'll happen is you'll ask off those accounts that have bad clients. If you're professional, you're not going to suddenly reach down to some guy who's a hack client that you know is only going to respond to mediocre stuff. You're going to still do the best you can. You've got to ram it down his throat.

An associate creative director

For good clients, all of your energy, all of your thought, all of your creativity is devoted to creating the best possible advertising product for that client. For bad or inept clients, a lot of your energy is devoted to "How do I persuade this person this is right? What kind of compromises do I make for this idea to even have a remote chance of being bought, accepted and produced?" Your thinking is diverted.

A creative director

I like him very much, and in that liking there's a desire to do whatever we can do to help him.

A copywriter

If you are working with a good client who's open to good ideas, creative people want to work on that business, and I've found that you can't stop them from working. They just want to work on it and they'll come up with ideas that have not even been asked for—and they'll spend twice as much time on that account than what's showing up on the time sheets because they like the praise and they want to do well and they know the client is open to good ideas and they can be successful on a piece of business like that.

On pieces of business that have a horrible reputation with creative people, it's difficult to get them to work on it, and if they are assigned to it, they don't put one hundred percent into it. They'd rather be working on something they enjoy.

An account supervisor

If an agency does not create consistently good advertising for a company and does not provide an adequate level of service, it can, of course, be fired by that client. However, you don't want just good advertising, you want the *best,* and that requires that your agency people, especially the creative people, be devoted to you and your business success.

THE ADVERTISING AGENCY VERSUS OTHER VENDORS

The need to establish an ongoing personal as well as professional relationship is what makes working with an agency different from working with other vendors outside your company. There are other differences worth noting.

- You are dealing with an organization that has its own structure and politics, not just one person who is selling you something. You have to learn and understand the structure and politics involved.
- You are working with many different kinds of people. While the account people may have the same business background as you do, the creative people often have quite different goals and different lifestyles that take some getting used to.
- A tremendous amount of money will be behind the decisions you make about advertising—often in the millions of dollars. Those decisions aren't made and then forgotten. Your advertising appears in the media over and over again.
- Your decisions are highly visible.

Richard Rosenbloom, vice president of Advertising at the Card Division of American Express, put it most succinctly: "In the final analysis, the agency is a vendor, but the difference between the agency and other vendors is that intangible, fragile thing called creativity. A client must provide the environment that allows the agency to do what they do best."

The agency is your source of great advertising, but to use it well, you must establish the right chemistry, and the first step toward doing that is to understand what makes agencies tick.

NOTES—CHAPTER 1

1. William M. Claggett, "The Best and Worst in Advertiser-Agency Relationships" (New York: 1975 Annual Meeting, Association of National Advertisers, Inc.), p. 17.
2. *The Wall Street Journal,* June 18, 1987, p. 10.
3. Booz • Allen & Hamilton, Inc., *Management & Advertising Problems in the Advertiser-Agency Relationship* (New York: Association of National Advertisers, Inc., 1965), p. 33.
4. Marvin Bower, "Getting the Best Out of Your Advertising Agency" (New York: 1968 Annual Meeting, Association of National Advertisers, Inc.), p. 16.
5. Booz • Allen & Hamilton, Inc., *op. cit.,* p. 114.
6. Ibid., p. 65.

CASE 1.
The Disrespected Product Manager

YOU ARE: A product manager recently promoted from assistant product manager on the same product.

THE PROBLEM: The agency will not fully respect your new role. They fulfill assignments as requested, but they often disregard your comments on copy and media plans. They look instead to your boss, the group product manager, with whom they have been working for more than a year, for final decisions. She does not fully respect your new role, either, because she permits the agency to go over your head.

What should you do?

chapter 2

What makes agencies tick? The organization

Imagine yourself walking down Third Avenue in New York City. You're surrounded by 40-story, glass-walled office buildings on both sides of the street. All kinds of people are rushing around: men with briefcases, women with briefcases, delivery boys carrying leaky brown bags of coffee. Horns honk. Carbon monoxide fills the air. You turn right, push your way through a revolving door, and enter one of the buildings. You walk across the stone floor of the lobby to the elevators, step in, and suddenly find yourself surrounded by a dozen freckle-faced, redheaded eight-year-old girls, all smiling sweetly at you. The only explanation is that somewhere in that vast building there's an advertising agency holding a casting session!

Advertising agencies don't look or feel or sound like other businesses. They're often not very businesslike at all; they're far more colorful. Of course, typewriters type and telephones ring, but sometimes carpets are bright red or bright green. Walls are filled with advertisements of layer cakes and children brushing their teeth and cars speeding down treacherous roads. Some people are wearing jeans and casual weekend shirts. There is a disproportionate number of bearded men and arty-looking women as well as men and women in business suits. Some are carrying drawings and storyboards. Others are carrying video tape cassettes. Everyone seems to be walking quickly. The energy level is high.

Even in the reception area, an advertising agency feels alive, exciting. It's a glamorous, fascinating place to visit. In fact, it's more than that. It's *fun,* because at the heart of an advertising agency is creativity.

WHAT IS AN ADVERTISING AGENCY?

An advertising agency is a profit-making business whose tangible product is advertising: the creation of advertising, the production of advertising, and the placement of advertising. They are called agencies because they used to act as agents for the media in which the advertising was placed. They represented the media—radio, magazines, newspapers—to the companies that advertised, and their income was the commission paid to them by the media for their representation.

Agencies began by selling space in newspapers, usually to retail advertisers. Some agencies still perform only that placement function. However, recognizing that an advertiser who bought media needed the advertising itself to place in the media, agencies started to offer the services of advertising creation and production. Their purposes were to help their advertisers and to lure advertisers to place their media dollars through the agency. As creative and other services were added, the agencies became agents of the advertisers instead of the media.

AGENCY SERVICES: AN OVERVIEW

Virtually all of the largest advertising agencies are known as full-service agencies: J. Walter Thompson, Young & Rubicam, Ogilvy & Mather, BBDO, and so on. All offer their clients a wide range of services, including the four basic services: creative, account management/marketing, media, research. Let's look at each briefly to give you an overall perspective on the work of such an agency.

Creative.   The primary service of any advertising agency is to create and produce advertising to place in the media. The creation and production of advertising accounted for approximately one third of the payroll costs of AAAA member agencies in 1980. (See Table 1 on page 15.)

Account management/marketing.   In addition to representing the client within the agency and coordinating the agen-

TABLE 1
Payroll Costs as a Percentage of Total Payroll

AAAA Agencies—1980

	1980
Creative development and production	32.2%
Creative	(23.7)
Print prod./traffic	(5.8)
TV and radio prod./traffic	(2.7)
Contact (account management)	27.5
Executive overhead	9.0
Media	7.7
General office overhead	6.0
Accounting	6.4
New business	6.0
Research	2.7
Publicity and PR	2.3
Data processing	.2
Total	100.0%

Source: American Association of Advertising Agencies' annual analysis of agency costs. (Used by permission.)

cy's services for the client, the agency account management group often offers marketing analysis and advice. This service can range from a second opinion on marketing decisions being made by the advertiser to functioning as the marketing department of a smaller advertiser. In 1980, account management or "contact" services accounted for about 28 percent of AAAA member agencies' payrolls.

Media. All full-service agencies continue to perform the services upon which the agency business was built: the planning of how advertising budgets will be allocated and the purchase of the media. In 1980, AAAA member agencies spent approximately 8 percent of their payrolls on media.

Research. The planning, execution, and interpretation of marketing research are services also offered by full-service agencies. Usually the research conducted by the agency rather than the advertiser's research department concerns the relative effectiveness of advertising concepts and executions. Advertiser research departments tend to conduct the product research and the large attitude and usage studies. In 1980, AAAA member agencies spent about 3 percent of their payrolls on research.

Creative, account management/marketing, media, and research are the four basic services offered by advertising agencies. However, either through special departments or subsidiary agencies, some agencies offer other services, including packaging design, promotion development and execution, public relations, new product development, and specialized advertising, such as direct response and recruitment.

AGENCY ORGANIZATION AND SERVICES

An advertising agency is structured around the services it offers. Although organization can differ from agency to agency, basically the structure of a large agency looks like the diagram on page 17.

In most large agencies and some smaller ones, there is the position of chairman of the board. In large international agencies, there may be an international chairman and chairmen of each country or group of countries. The function of the chairperson is to provide overall direction for the work, growth, and management of the agency. He or she is rarely involved with the management of individual clients unless there are major problems.

The president of the agency, who is a member of the board, is more involved with individual clients because one of his major responsibilities is the allocation of agency resources to service the clients. How agency resources are allocated in large part determines an agency's profitability. Presidents are also often responsible for the acquisition of new business and may be involved in the overall management of some of the agency's larger accounts.

Chairmen and presidents of advertising agencies usually arrive at their positions via the creative or account management routes. Those agency leaders with creative backgrounds include David Ogilvy, Ogilvy & Mather; Mary Wells, Wells

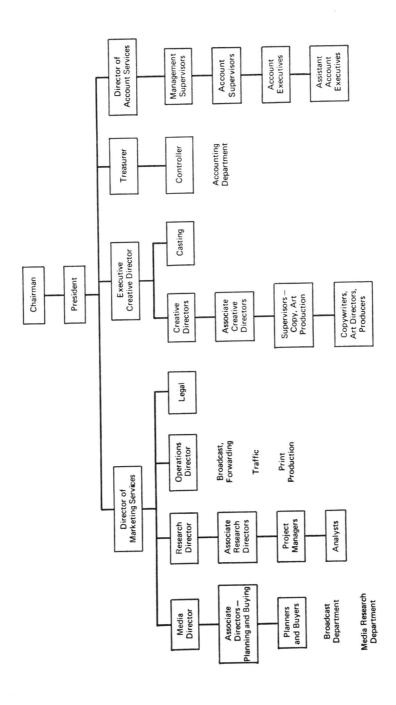

Chairman

President

Director of Marketing Services

Executive Creative Director

Treasurer

Director of Account Services

Media Director

Associate Directors — Planning and Buying

Planners and Buyers

Broadcast Department

Media Research Department

Research Director

Associate Research Directors

Project Managers

Analysts

Operations Director

Broadcast, Forwarding

Traffic

Print Production

Legal

Creative Directors

Associate Creative Directors

Supervisors — Copy, Art Production

Copywriters, Art Directors, Producers

Casting

Controller

Accounting Department

Management Supervisors

Account Supervisors

Account Executives

Assistant Account Executives

Rich Greene; Allen Rosenshine, Omnicom Group. Those with account management backgrounds include Donald Johnston of J. Walter Thompson; Kenneth Roman and William Phillips, Ogilvy & Mather; Marvin Sloves, Scali, McCabe, Sloves.

The board of directors is composed of the senior officers of the agency, who are usually the heads of departments and heads of larger accounts or groups of accounts. The function of an agency board of directors is virtually the same as that of any board of directors: to make the major decisions regarding organization, direction, growth, and profitability.

The executive creative director is responsible for all of the creative work developed and produced by the agency. It is his or her job to keep the standards of the work high, to make certain that the advertising is effective and that it is work of which both the advertiser and agency can feel proud. The executive creative director must usually see and approve all new campaigns before they are shown to the advertisers. In medium-sized and small agencies, the executive creative director will see every advertisement before it is presented.

Reporting to the executive creative director are subsidiary departments that aid in the creation and production of advertising. These include casting, music (in larger agencies only), and television production, if it is a separate department. Also reporting to the executive creative director are creative directors, with their own staffs of writers, art directors, and producers. (In some agencies, producers report to a director of production but are assigned to an individual creative director.)

Creative directors are assigned specific accounts within the agency with which they will often work for many years, so as to establish continuity with the marketing and advertising problems of a particular product or service and with the people working for the advertiser company. Sometimes creative directors are assigned accounts according to their special talents (long, informative copy, for example) or the needs of a special type of client. All drug products may be under the supervision of one creative director because of the unique way consumers respond to drug advertising and the many legal restrictions involved in its creation. Other specialties include financial advertising, banks and stock brokerage firms, and fashion advertising.

The copywriters and art directors, copy supervisors, and art supervisors who report to the creative directors usually work in teams. They collaborate—tossing ideas back and forth until a basic point of view for the advertisement is created. In a print advertisement, the point of view might include the major visual and the headline. In a commercial, it will include the situation and rough copy. After the point of view is created, the writer and art director will often work alone on polishing the final layout and copy of the advertising.

Copywriter-art director teams are also assigned to individual accounts for an extended period of time. Teams must learn about the product or service, the competition, and the attitudes and usage habits of the consumers to whom their advertising is addressed. There is often a point of diminishing returns on the number of exciting, motivating ideas a creative team can develop for one product or service. Creative talent may stay fresh and alive, but it can wear out on a particular account. Therefore, creative teams will usually change accounts more often than the creative director, sometimes as often as every nine months. The creative director provides the important continuity.

Once a print advertisement is approved for production, it is the art director's job to hire an illustrator or photographer, specify the typeface, oversee the making of the mechanical, and in general prepare the advertisement for engraving. The actual engraving will be given on contract by the print-production department to a company outside the agency that specializes in engraving. Once a television or radio commercial is approved for production, it becomes the responsibility of the agency producer. She makes it come alive. She initiates the casting process, hires music composers and arrangers, if needed, and contracts with a commercial production company outside the agency to produce the television commercial. Radio commercials are often produced by the agency's own producer.

Once an advertisement or commercial is completed and ready to be released to the publication or broadcast media, the agency's creative process is completed.

As discussed briefly in Chapter 1, the account management group is often structured to mirror the organization of the advertiser. The purpose is to give each level an agency counterpart with the same level of expertise and responsibility on whom he can call. Management supervisors work with the director of marketing or, in a small advertiser, the president of the company. Account supervisors work with the group product managers, and so forth. For advertisers with more complex levels of responsibility, agencies may assign two levels of account supervisors, one with a vice president's title and one without. In some cases, an account may have two management supervisors: the vice president, management supervisor reports to a senior vice president, management supervisor. In large agencies with many management supervisors, they all might report to a director of account services instead of directly to the president.

The major responsibility of a management supervisor is to manage the agency services needed on her account so that her clients receive the best possible service at the least cost to the agency. She strives to make her accounts productive and profitable. A management supervisor may oversee one large account that has many products assigned to the agency or one division of a large account. For smaller clients, a management supervisor may handle several accounts.

Management supervisors usually remain on their accounts for many years, and do not leave unless they change agencies, advertiser personnel changes, or in rare instances, some personal disagreement develops with the client. If a management supervisor is promoted to executive vice president or even president, she will usually maintain some level of responsibility for the account on which she was management supervisor. In fact, management supervisors have often risen through the ranks of a given account from the level of account executive. They are often the strongest people who have worked on an account and who remained as the pyramid became narrower. Therefore, the management supervisor will have had in-depth experience with the client company and the history of client products and the markets in which they compete.

While the management supervisor manages the agency resources, the function of the account supervisor is to manage the account—to provide the basic direction for the advertising, media, and marketing work prepared by the agency. This individual tries to anticipate a client's advertising and marketing needs, and to anticipate those needs so that the agency is guiding rather than responding to direction from the advertiser. He also will supervise all the day-to-day work of the accounts he manages.

Account supervisors often have responsibility for at least two accounts and may remain on those accounts for two or more years. In keeping an account supervisor on a given account, agency management tries to balance the importance of continuity with the need to give broad management experience with different types of businesses. An account supervisor may remain at that level for three to five years. Often, a vice presidency title is conferred after two or three years.

Basically, an account executive gets things done. She makes certain that the creative teams are creating, that the media planners are planning, and that production is proceeding on time and within the budget.

Unlike the account supervisor, the account executive may be assigned only one account, if that account is large enough. The purpose is to provide her with the time to know her client's business almost as well as her client does. This knowledge includes production, pricing, packaging, sales—everything that can help make the agency's work, both advertising and marketing, effective and implementable.

An account executive will usually be assigned to an account for one or two years before being transferred to gain experience in a different category and with a different client company. A good account executive can be expected to be promoted after two to three years.

An assistant account executive is responsible for the more routine aspects of account management: preparing and maintaining budgets, billing, estimates for production and media, analyzing marketing data, media expenditures, and competitive advertising. He may remain at the assistant account executive level for anywhere from six months to two years, during which time he may work on one or two accounts.

In large agencies, a director of marketing services coordinates four departments: media, marketing research, operations, and legal. We'll review media first.

The media department of an agency performs three basic functions: planning, buying, and research. The planning function is the largest, and has the levels of supervisor, planner, and assistant planner. Media people are assigned to specific accounts and, at the supervisory level, may remain on those accounts for many years for the purpose of providing continuity with the client's business and personnel. The media people who work directly with advertisers determine, within given budget levels, the objectives and strategy for media spending, the media in which the money will be spent, the geographic areas where it will be spent, how often, and against which target audience.

(NOTE: The preceding paragraph gives an overview of a highly complex and critical area of marketing and advertising. Although media is only a small part of the actual creative process of advertising development, it is, nevertheless, an important part of working with your agency. Media is not within the scope of this book; however, many excellent books have been written on the subject and many excellent courses and seminars, including one by the ANA, are given throughout the country.)

The media department also purchases space and time. The cost of media space in magazines, newspapers, and supplements is set by the publications in their rate cards. Usually print media do not negotiate prices; therefore, at most agencies, media planners are also the buyers of print space. However, broadcast time on radio and television is usually negotiated. Therefore, people who are skilled in negotiating perform the buying function. Buying is further divided into radio buyers, spot-television buyers, and network-television buyers. Because of the amount of money involved in purchasing network-television time, this function is often handled by a separate division of the media department called *broadcast*. However, many advertiser companies choose to purchase network time themselves; this function will be a responsibility of the advertising vice president.

Another function of most media departments is media research. This division coordinates all of the services available to aid media planning and evaluation, including competitive spending data, rating data, and analysis of industry developments, such as cable television.

The function of marketing research is to plan, execute, and interpret research. For some advertisers, this service will include attitude and usage research of the product category and segmentation studies. These studies are background research providing direction for all marketing functions. For other advertisers, research will center around the effectiveness of advertising positionings and executions. Some larger advertisers do not use agency research departments, preferring to use their own research department in all areas.

Agency research departments will plan research and often write questionnaires. They will then contract with an outside supplier to actually conduct the research in the field. At the completion of the research, results will be forwarded to the agency research department, which will then interpret the data. Structurally, the agency research department has supervisory, director, and assistant levels similar to those in media.

The operations area encompasses many separate departments within an agency without which advertising would never be produced or delivered on time. Included in the operations area are:

Traffic. Traffic's sole job is to know dates of magazine closings, television air dates, and to physically move around the agency making certain all departments do their jobs so that dates are not missed and all approvals are obtained. Traffic people are also responsible for knowing whether work is being completed within the estimated budget. A traffic person must be extremely well organized and know how to persist without becoming a nag.

Print production. This department is responsible for preparing all the materials required by the print media (magazines, newspapers, and supplements). It is a complex operation because magazines and newspapers are produced in a variety of sizes and use different printing processes. Agency print-production departments will contract with outside engravers to prepare materials for publications. They will also oversee the printing process for collateral material, such as brochures.

Broadcast forwarding. As the name suggests, this department is responsible for ordering broadcast films and tapes and delivering them to the right stations or networks across the country. For some advertisers, this function can be as simple as sending tapes to ABC, NBC, and CBS. For others (airlines, for example, which have routes between specific cities and which change their advertising every few weeks to announce new rates), the job can be staggering, involving as it does dozens of cities and hundreds of stations.

Legal. Some large agencies maintain their own staff of lawyers to advise on the legality of copy and to keep the agency up-to-date on industry, government, and media regulations of advertising.

Finance. The financial people—treasurer, controller, accounting department—perform a crucial role in overseeing the agency's profitability and guarding the agency's cash flow. Because of the agency's function as middleman—buying the media and, in effect, being reimbursed by the advertiser—cash flow is always a problem. During periods of high interest rates and slow payment of bills, it's not surprising that many agencies find themselves in difficult cash-flow situations; so the functions of the finance department become all that much more important.

AGENCY COMPENSATION

The method of agency compensation used frequently by major advertisers is the commission system, in which an agency's billings are the gross amount of money spent by the advertiser, and the agency's income is the difference between the cost of the media to the advertiser and the cost of the media to the agency. Although always negotiable, this usually delivers a commission of 15 percent of the gross to the agency. Under the commission system, production is also marked up—17.65 percent to deliver a commission to the agency that is 15 percent of the gross.

There are two other methods of agency compensation. Both involve either partial or total use of a fee. On a straight-fee system, the advertiser pays the net cost of the media, the same price the agency pays, but all agency time spent on the account is marked up to ensure the agency a certain percentage of profit, sometimes as low as 10 percent and sometimes as high as 25 percent.

The other method of agency compensation is a combination of fee and commission. Under this system, if agency costs including profit are below what the commission would be, agency and client split the remaining commission in some agreed-upon way. If agency expenses exceed the commission, agency costs and profit are covered as in a straight-fee arrangement.

If you do not know how your agency is compensated, you should find out. An agency's ability to provide services to an advertiser is somewhat determined by the method of compensation. For example, the cost of a special creative assignment would be assumed by the advertiser under a fee arrangement, but would affect agency profits under a commission arrangement.

HOW AGENCIES MAKE MONEY

Advertising agencies make a profit the same way any other business does: on the difference between their income and the cost of producing their product or service.

With advertising agencies, however, the cost-of-goods is determined mostly by the cost of the "machinery," that is, the people who manage the process and produce the advertising, and overhead. There are really no other costs except those for production, and they are usually borne by the advertiser. The cost of creating advertising for you is determined, therefore, by the salaries of the people assigned to your business, the amount of time they need to create your advertising, plus a factor for overhead.

Around the start of each year, the management supervisor, or whoever is responsible for the profit on your account, will work with her people, and often with you too, to determine both the amount of work they will be doing for you and the projected yearly income to the agency.

It is important that you recognize that to do their best work for you, agencies need to make a profit. Obviously, it is a key motivation of any profit-making organization. Infringing too much on agency profit can seriously affect the quality of your advertising. Buying the services of an advertising agency is not like getting a good deal on a car. Presumably the quality of the car stays the same no matter what you pay; however, if you cut too deeply into projected agency profit on your account, both the advertising and the service will suffer.

> Recognizing that profitable agencies do the best work and that profitable agency margins are very thin today, marketing managers need to sensitize their brand management teams to the risks involved in demanding service beyond the strategic thinking for, and the execution and placement of, major advertising campaigns *if* the added work significantly reduces the profitability of the account. The costs of doing additional work without additional compensation siphon quality people's time away from the brand's main advertising efforts. The internal pressure on account management to keep the business profitable includes substantial impact on their income from bonus and profit sharing and most of them will act to reasonably protect their interests.
>
> *F. Kent Mitchel, President of the Marketing Science Institute and former Director of Marketing Staffs, General Foods*

Your relationship with your agency is also important to their profitability. To quote Allen Rosenshine, President and CEO, Omnicom Group, "Agencies make money by providing services efficiently. Getting it right as early in the process as possible is not only better for the advertiser, it contributes to profitability. Under most compensation arrangements, the more revisions and versions, the less money the agency makes. At the heart of 'getting it right' is a good professional relationship. Additionally, the relationship is directly related to profitability because it allows the agency to tell the advertiser that it is making either too little or too much money. Many fees are predicated on the agency making neither."

AGENCY SIZE

As with many things in life, size has little to do with performance. Tiny agencies can create great advertising. Huge mega-agencies can create great advertising. The reason is that all it takes to create great advertising—in addition, of course, to a skillful advertiser—is an account executive who understands your business, plus a talented copywriter and art director team. They form the core group that develops your advertising at a large agency, and they may be the only group at a small agency.

Additionally, the factors found necessary to obtain great advertising in the Salz Survey of the top 200 advertisers and top 100 agencies (see Appendix)—the skills of the people, setting high standards, agency people wanting to work on your business, good communication, and minimal advertiser-approval levels—are not size-dependent.

According to the survey, even the huge agency mergers that took place during 1986 (the Omnicom Group, the Saatchi & Saatchi acquisitions and mergers) did not affect the quality of the advertising among those advertisers and agencies still working together.

However, advertisers don't just go to an agency for the development of advertising. Often they want and need other services, such as media, research, promotion, direct response, public relations, and international coordination of their advertising. When these services are needed, size does become a factor. Small agencies, those with billings of under $5 to $6 million, often cannot afford the staffs to provide many of these services, although the *quality* of the services they do provide may be the same.

The size of your agency should mainly be determined by the size of your total advertising budget, the size of your individual agency assignments, and the types of services you require.

Here's how Du Pont, one of the world's largest companies and advertisers, determined that on many of their businesses a relatively small agency was better for them than a large agency. According to Lee C. Tashjian, Jr., Director of Communications at E. I. du Pont de Nemours & Company:

"We saw a problem with some of our large agencies, and we saw it as our fault. With a large number of product lines all at one agency there was no way that they could understand all of our businesses. They couldn't be reactive, participative or imaginative the way they wanted to be and the way we wanted them to be. Over time, the service became marginal due mainly to the volume of work and the smaller budgets associated with many of these products. Further complicating things was considerable pressure within Du Pont to put stronger limits on ever increasing agency fees. Along the way, we even tried copy contacts instead of account people to keep costs down, but they could not provide the much needed marketing or strategic input. We felt that this situation was a poor use of our money and created a very difficult situation for the agency.

"So we decided to disengage a number of our industrial businesses from larger agencies—provided that the creative work could be the same. We looked at many local agencies and have hired a few of them. We've found that the creative product is as good and sometimes better. We are getting better service. Our people are happier. And we're saving a considerable amount of money."

The bottom line is, when it comes to the quality of the advertising, the results of working with a large agency can be essentially the same as working with a small agency. No matter what its size, *people* create the advertising. They have the same skills, the same approach to the process. They may even be the same people because talented teams from large agencies often leave to form their own agencies, and new agencies are usually small to start.

Therefore, no matter what the size of your agency, you need the same important understanding and skills if you want to get the best possible advertising.

Now that you understand something of the structural backbone of an advertising agency, let's look at the copywriters, art directors, account group, and officers, and learn what makes agency *people* tick.

CASE 2.
The Disrespected Account Executive

YOU ARE: The owner of a small business.
THE PROBLEM: The agency has just assigned a newly promoted account executive to your account. He's bright; he's learning your business, but he hasn't earned the respect of the agency creative and media people. The direction you and he have agreed to is not being followed. What should you do?

CASE 3.
About-Face!

YOU ARE: An advertising manager at a large company working with a large agency.

THE PROBLEM: The agency has just presented four television campaigns for your company, one of which they are excited about and you think is the best advertising ever done for your business. The presentation, attended by the agency account supervisor, account executive, copywriter, and art director, took place the previous week. You have lived with the campaigns for a few days, and, if some minor revisions are made, you are ready to present to your own marketing and product groups.

When you phone the account executive to arrange the next presentation, she tells you that the agency has changed its mind about the campaign you all loved. They no longer want to proceed with it. They would be happy to present the other three campaigns but would prefer to create some additional advertising and return in a week.

What is going on here? What should you do?

chapter 3

What makes
agencies tick?
The people

A client has to understand that what makes agencies tick is bright, hungry people who want to work on his business. They've got to want to.

J. Leonard Hultgren, founding partner,
Scali, McCabe, Sloves

In Chapter 1, we covered what you expect from great advertising and why it's important to your business and your career. When you're managing your agency and all the different kinds of people assigned to your business, you need to understand why they want great advertising too—what it means to them personally and professionally. If you become an advertiser with whom agency people want to work, you will be an advertiser who gets the best advertising from his agency.

AGENCY MANAGEMENT

The motivation of advertising-agency management is similar to the motivation of any management—the recognition of having reached the top; the money, power, and control that go along with it; and becoming the leading organization in their field. This leads us to ask, how does agency management define success and what kind of advertiser helps them achieve it?

Agency management defines success primarily by the advertising their agency creates. They want clients who encourage the agency to do its best work and produce superior advertising—advertising that not only sells their clients' products and services but also represents work of which they can be proud. Naturally, they want advertising that is recognized as great by other advertisers so that it attracts new business to the agency. They also want to create advertising that is recognized as great by other agencies, that's covered in the press, that wins awards—advertising that attracts bright, talented people to the agency because they know it's a place where they'll want to work. An agency's reputation is primarily determined by the quality of the advertising it produces. Of course, it may also be known for the quality of its clients, for its marketing counsel and media expertise, but without great advertising the agency cannot become great.

The importance of any client to an agency is also related to the amount of profit the agency produces on that client's business. For some reason, advertisers, especially at the junior level, who spend most of their time trying to increase profits on their own business, tend to forget that agencies have the same profit motives they do. Of course, profits may be sacrificed to invest in a new client who will be profitable in the future or less-profitable clients for whom the agency can produce advertising that showcases the agency's creativity, but in many agencies, especially those that are publicly held, profits are almost equal in importance to producing outstanding advertising.

Success to agency management may also be defined by the importance of the advertisers served. Important can mean:

- Large, famous companies—Exxon, Procter & Gamble, Johnson & Johnson, General Motors.
- Companies, both large and small, that are leaders in their fields—Steinway Pianos, Rolls-Royce.
- Small, prestigious companies with products or services that cater to influential consumers.

Thus, agencies are known by the size and fame of their clients as well as by the advertising produced for them. It is success by association with success. You may never have heard of a relatively new agency called Backer & Spielvogel, but you've heard of two of their major clients, Miller Beer and Campbell Soup.

Smaller, prestigious advertisers are important to an agency because the advertising created for them is directed at consumers who could be future clients of the agency. Many agencies would covet the Morgan Guaranty account because the advertising would be targeted to corporation presidents and chairmen who are in a position to give the agency their future advertising business.

A growing agency is a successful agency. There is little that is more exciting and "sexy" to the management of any agency, large or small, than the words "new business." For large agencies, new clients enable them to grow larger and make more money. No matter how large an agency is, new business proves to its management that the agency is important and desirable.

Finally, agency success is defined by the calibre of its people, an agency's only asset. They are the means of production, and the brighter, more talented, more energetic an agency's people, the better the advertising and service the agency can produce.

Of course, all the previous factors discussed contribute to an agency's ability to attract and hold good people. The better the advertising, the more the talented people will want to work at the agency because they feel they will be able to produce their best work there. The more profitable the agency, the more it can afford to pay and hold on to good people. The larger the advertisers, the more visible will be the people who created their advertising. The more an agency grows, the more opportunities it can offer its people for advancement and diversity of assignment.

In sum, agency management wants great advertising, high profits, some important clients, growth, and bright, talented people.

ACCOUNT MANAGEMENT

Account management people are more like you in their lifestyles and business responsibilities than other advertising employees are like you. They are managers, marketers, coordinators. Many have MBA's, yet they chose the agency side rather than the advertiser side. Why? A few reasons:

They are often problem solvers and enjoy the analysis-solution process. Above all, they are excited by good ideas, and they would rather produce an idea than a product or service. They are stimulated by creativity, the creative process, and creative people—often in music, art, theater, literature, as well as advertising. They enjoy the diversity of working on different products every year or so—or, at higher levels, on different products simultaneously. They enjoy making the marketing decisions that help sell the product or service to customers— positioning, strategy—but they find other areas of the marketing process, particularly manufacturing, sales, and promotion, somewhat boring.

Understanding the motivation of account people is a bit more difficult than understanding advertisers, agency management, or creative people. It would be helpful to start by recognizing two aspects of their roles. First, account managers are middlemen. Their job is to understand your business, develop an advertising point of view with you, and communicate that point of view to the creative people, as well as understand the creative point of view and communicate that back to you. Although often debated, it is generally agreed that the role of account management is necessitated in part by the different perspectives brought to the advertising problem by the advertiser and the creative people. According to Jane Steele Kaufman, advertising manager of Steuben Glass, "To me, the account executive doesn't just write the memos; she's the person who understands what's going on. . . . In order for her to solve any problem for us, she has to know how to communicate the aspects of the problem to the rest of the agency. . . . It has to do with having an overview—seeing the forest as well as the trees."

The second aspect of the account management role you should recognize is that, in effect, account managers have two bosses: you, the advertiser, and their own agency boss. Many times, being successful with clients will gain account people success with agency superiors. However, account people can frequently find themselves in the difficult position of trying to satisfy two bosses who do not agree with each other. Therefore, given their role as middlemen and frequent reconcilers of two bosses' views, what do account managers want?

Account managers want to sell your product for you. They want to understand your consumers and competitors so as to position your product, develop your advertising strategy, and stimulate the creative people to produce outstanding advertising. They want to perform that aspect of your job that interests them the most without becoming involved in those aspects of the job they may find boring! So after account people have solved your positioning and strategic problems, they want to work with creative people to help them develop outstanding advertising. That means presenting the marketing problem in a way that will stimulate the creative people, supporting them emotionally and intellectually as they work through the creative process and then see the end result of great advertising.

Necessary to achieving their goals of selling an advertiser's product and creating outstanding advertising is an advertiser with whom an account person can work well. An account manager defines a good client as a client who is helped, not threatened, by the agency's ideas, who is trying to sell his product or service more than just gain his superior's approval, and who is effective within the advertiser company so that the ideas presented by the agency are conveyed and implemented.

Like you, account managers want to advance. The pressures to move up the ladder within the agency are as strong as the pressures on the advertiser side. Agency account people are known as much by their contributions to the growth of their client's business as the advertiser is.

Finally, account managers want to be effective managers of people. That means creating an atmosphere in which creative, media, and all support groups enjoy working on their account(s), and, therefore, produce superior work and results.

> I receive the greatest satisfaction from my job when I see a project through from beginning to end. Understanding the problem, developing a strategy, involving the creative people, seeing the advertising, finally getting it approved, and then seeing the results of months or even years of work. It's very exciting.
>
> *Susan Hudson, Vice President, Account*
> *Supervisor, Ogilvy & Mather*

CREATIVE

The creative mind and the creative process have fascinated scholars for centuries. Many have developed theories to explain how an idea comes into being. Even creative people themselves have trouble understanding the process.

> I don't know how I do what I do. It's not completely under control.
> . . . All I know is if I worry about it, I can't do it. If I don't worry
> about it, I can do it.
>
> *A copywriter*

Creative people in advertising are similar to creative people in literature, art, music, theater, and film in that they search for fresh, new perspectives on existing information. By using their intuition, imagination, and logical thought processes, they invent ideas. According to Booz • Allen & Hamilton, "The 'idea' and its use are their absorption—and management's interest in company profit is almost uninteresting to them. They are much like their counterparts in the applied research side of R&D."[1]

However, creative people in advertising may differ from creative people in other areas in several important ways. They are stimulated by the reality of the business world, by seeing the end result of consumer reaction to their work in the form of sales, and they prefer to work on small projects that take days or weeks to create rather than months or years. Think of the differences between a single-page advertisement and a book, or a 30-second commercial and a film. Moreover, creative people enjoy seeing their work produced and appearing in the media where millions of people see it. A successful paperback book is read by 4 or 5 million people. A commercial for a major product can be seen by 100 million people in a few weeks. Most importantly, they enjoy creating to stimulate an end result rather than creating for its own sake.

Because creating ideas that solve advertising problems is their primary job, creative people are of necessity shielded by the account group from the day-to-day problems that confront any account. Creative people should be unencumbered so that they can focus all of their intellectual and emotional abilities on the major pieces of the advertising puzzle: the product, the competition, and the consumer. They must totally immerse themselves in the product or service, consumer attitudes toward it and usage of it, and create one simple idea that, when presented to consumers, will make them want to buy the product or service.

Creating an idea doesn't just happen between the hours of

nine and five. Creative people live the problem, feel it, all the time.

> I'm completely the opposite of the punch clock. My work is all the time. . . . If somebody said "give a little thought to this in the shower one morning," I'd have to say, "I'm sorry, my showers are all booked up for the next month."
>
> *Jeff Atlas, Copywriter, Ogilvy & Mather*

Because of their total immersion in the creation of advertising, creative people are personally a part of the advertising they create, and in the last analysis, advertising needs that investment of personal feeling to be effective. Consumers buy from a gut or emotional reaction more than from the sway of logic, so without that emotional element, advertising would read like a creative strategy and never motivate anyone to buy. For example, note the difference between these two statements:

Federal Express will give you overnight service.
versus
Federal Express: when it absolutely, positively has to be there overnight.

Given all of the emotional involvement and full-time thinking, why do creative people go into advertising in the first place? What do they want?

They want to produce great advertising—effective advertising of which they are proud—and have some fun and glory along the way. Here are some remarks that explain:

> The greatest reward is to have something that everyone acknowledges as a terrific solution to the problem—unique, different.
>
> *Malcolm End, Senior Vice President,*
> *Creative Director, Ogilvy & Mather*

> That's the mark of an advertising professional. If you're a dilettante, you want to do nice ads for yourself and for your portfolio. The ad is an end in itself. But really the results are the end of the ad. There has to be the satisfaction of solving the thing elegantly but in a way that will produce results.
>
> *Bernard Rosner, Vice President, Creative Director,*
> *Ogilvy & Mather Partners*

I remember when I was thirteen and my father and Walter Weir were sitting in the living room. A bottle of liquor was on the mantel. They were looking at the bottle, they were looking at the label, thinking about ads, what they could do to sell it. They were having fun. And I knew from that time on that that's what I wanted to do. I wanted to have the kind of fun they were having if I had to make a living at something. . . . I don't think I could write long, to be honest. I don't think I have those kinds of ideas—no "great American novels" in me. Hopefully, I've got great American ads. And I like it. I just like it. I find it very fulfilling.

Bob Neuman, Senior Vice President, Associate Creative
Director, Backer & Spielvogel

What's fun about it? Example: my art director and I, we thought of this ad. I saw this in my head—a girl in a pool. And we sketched it out. And it became real. Well, not too many people get a chance to have their dreams made real. That's what we do: We get our dreams made real, and that's pretty neat.

A copywriter

You certainly want money . . . because there's a need for income. . . . I found a route to earn money that I enjoy doing. There may be areas to earn more that I wouldn't enjoy as much. I think there's a good balance. . . . There's more of a progression up the corporate ladder for clients. That is distinctly different from the creative department. Most people in creative are happy to do what they're doing and would be happy doing that forever. Art directors want to be art directors and copywriters want to be copywriters. A few may want to be managers, but they're usually thrust into that circumstance by the upward pressure of salary. As you get higher and higher, you take on more administrative responsibilities to justify your salary. . . . I see doing the work, and doing it happily, and getting good results as a worthwhile end.

An associate creative director

Our greatest reward is closing the door and throwing a lot of paper in the wastebasket till we get a satisfying idea.

Franchellie Cadwell, President, and Herman Davis,
Executive Vice President and Creative Director,
Cadwell Davis Partners

There's a part of advertising that gives me the greatest satisfaction and after that it's all downhill. That's the initial conception stage. If I'm just working with an art director on something and we get an idea that solves the problem, that's the most satisfying part.

A copywriter

You've got to satisfy yourself in terms of doing what you think is a first-rate job of solving the marketing problem to your own satisfaction. Not to anybody else's *yet*. First and foremost to yourself. That's where the kick comes.

Bernard Rosner, Vice President, Creative Director,
Ogilvy & Mather Partners

I'll never forget the first time an ad I'd written ran. It was for the British Travel Association and it ran in the Sunday travel section of the *New York Times*. I told everyone about it, including my grandmother. She bought the paper, then called me up, literally in tears. "If you wrote it, why isn't your name on it?" she wanted to know. "It doesn't work that way," I told her. But I also realized that she was right. My name should have been there, in small, light type on the bottom of the ad, just like a photographer's credit.

A copywriter

There's a nice ego stroking that never stops. . . . When you stop enjoying seeing your work produced, something's wrong.

Bob Neuman, Senior Vice President, Associate
Creative Director, Backer & Speilvogel

For the advertiser, an advertisement that doesn't run has no use. For an agency creative person, there is satisfaction just in the process, and an outstanding advertisement that is not approved by the advertiser for some reason can still help a creative person within the agency. An advertisement that is produced but never runs can become a part of the creative person's portfolio, and help him get a better job.

The importance of these produced advertisements is best illustrated by a junior copywriter at one of the larger agencies. When he was told to evacuate his office because of a fire, instead of grabbing his coat he grabbed his portfolio!

If you stop for a moment here to review what advertisers,

agency management, account management, and creative people want from the client-agency relationship, you'll realize they all want the same result: great advertising. If everyone wants the same result, why is it so difficult to obtain? In the next chapter, we'll explore the reasons why as well as how to create the relationship with your agency that produces great advertising.

NOTE—CHAPTER 3

1. Booz • Allen & Hamilton, Inc., *Management & Advertising Problems in the Advertiser-Agency Relationship* (New York: Association of National Advertisers, Inc., 1965), p. 37.

CASE 4.
The Dictator

YOU ARE: A management supervisor at an advertising agency.
THE PROBLEM: A product manager, recently promoted onto a brand that advertises from a brand that doesn't, has gotten far too involved in the advertising. Her lack of experience, plus a very controlling personality, has caused her to write headlines, write body copy, rearrange layouts, and insist that her exact copy and layouts be implemented. This has been going on for six months.

The product manager likes the advertising; however, all at the agency believe that the advertising reads like a marketing plan, has too many visual elements, lacks humanity and, therefore, impact. The product manager refuses to spend the money to test it.

Your personal discussions with her have been fruitless. Your discussions with her boss and even the director of the division have also not helped. Both do not want to be involved, preferring the product manager to learn on the job.

The creative director at your agency has just substituted a junior copywriter-art director team for your usual team because he can put the senior team's talent to more productive use.

If the product manager is happy, why are you so concerned? What should you do?

CASE 5.
Possessiveness

YOU ARE: Director of advertising at a medium-sized company.
THE PROBLEM: The agency has assigned two creative teams to your business. One team is very good; the other is great. You would like to have the best team handle all of your business. It would mean they worked only on your account and no other. That idea pleases you, as you feel they would be able to think constantly about your business. Should you make this request?

chapter 4

The collaborative relationship: What it is and why it produces the best advertising

On the surface, it seems that developing a relationship that produces outstanding advertising should be easy, especially because all participants are personally and professionally committed to the same goal. However, the problems arise because the three groups of people who must work together in the creative process—advertiser, account management, and creative—all bring their own perspectives to the process and all have subjective definitions of what ought to be "effective advertising with which they are proud to be associated." Instead of pooling their ideas, often they are all pulling the advertising in their own directions.

This conflict is evident in the two extremes of how advertisers and agencies can work together. When an advertiser dominates the relationship, hires the agencies, pays the bills, and is ultimately responsible for the advertising decisions, it feels the agency should do things its way. Obversely, when the agency dominates the relationship, as the professional advertising expert, the agency feels the advertiser should follow the agency's directives. Obviously, neither relationship will produce superior advertising. In the first case, the advertiser isn't utilizing the talent of the agency, and in the latter instance, the agency isn't utilizing the expertise of the advertiser/client.

The relationship producing the best advertising is one that recognizes that each participant—advertiser, creative, and account management—must be a contributor to the common goal. In this relationship, agency and advertiser lines are forgotten, and it becomes a relationship of collaboration, people working together to produce a result that none could have achieved alone.

Booz • Allen & Hamilton cited the importance of collaboration in a study commissioned by the ANA. "Successful collaboration has been found to be the key to creativity and effective advertising."[1]

THE SUCCESSFUL COLLABORATION

A solid, working collaboration is almost always a struggle to achieve. It's easier to define: A successful collaboration is one in which each participant contributes from his own area of expertise and gains the satisfaction of seeing his contribution in the final result.

Let's look at a successful advertiser-agency collaboration: the development of advertising for the line extension of a leading health and beauty aid product. (A razor will be substituted for the actual product. The real advertiser prefers to remain anonymous.) The collaboration proceeded as follows.

The product manager invented the idea for a razor with a head that was larger than the original razor marketed by the brand. He analyzed consumer attitudes and concluded that although many men liked the original razor with its extra-small shaving head, others rejected the razor for the same reason. The company's group product manager endorsed the new larger-headed razor, but recognized a problem immediately, which he discussed with his advertising agency account supervisor. He questioned how the brand could explain the benefits of a larger-headed razor without denigrating the original razor.

The account supervisor, after discussing the problem with creative and other account people, developed a general perspective: The new larger-headed razor should not be advertised by itself; its major benefit, the larger head, was not unique to the category. Instead, the new razor should be introduced in the context of advertising that explained all the features of the razor, not just the head size. The agency creative team furthered the solution by developing a hypothesis: The razors seem to fit the face differently, and, because men have differently shaped faces, there may be a benefit associated with face shape and the fit of the razor.

Research and development confirmed that there was a benefit: The better a razor fits the face, the easier it is to shave. So, the agency-account group drafted a copy strategy. Creative people and the advertiser both made changes that improved upon it. Afterward, the copywriter and art director collaborated separately and created a television commercial which was tested and received the highest persuasion score in the brand's history. Six months after the commercial aired, the brand became number one in the category.

Now, who created the advertising? The creative people? The account people? The product group? They *all* did. They *collaborated,* and in the end, each person had the satisfaction of seeing his contribution in the successful result. The collaboration worked because of the special relationship and chemistry that existed among the collaborators. If we analyze that relationship, we'll see that there were six elements that *made* it work.

1. The collaborators continually focused on their common goal.
2. Their roles were clearly defined.
3. They were experts in their own areas and therefore earned the other collaborators' respect.
4. They trusted each other.
5. Client authority lines were relaxed.
6. The collaborators felt free to contribute in areas other than their own and accept suggestions from others in their own areas.

1. Focusing on the Common Goal

Although all collaborators want great advertising, they are bringing subjective views to the goal. Great advertising to an art director could mean photographing a car on top of a butte in Monument Valley at sunset. Great advertising to a copywriter could mean a clever headline. Great advertising to an advertiser could mean showing his package for the entire commercial and stating the product benefit seven times. It's this subjective definition of great advertising and pulling at the advertising to achieve an individual goal that makes it easy for collaborators to lose sight of their common goal. Professionals never stop trying.

> Successful advertising people—brand managers, account executives, and creative people—share one common characteristic: They are dedicated to making the product a marketing success. They see the big picture . . . where the pieces must fit to make the product successful. Conversely, people who fail in advertising see narrowly—like art directors who are primarily interested in aesthetics, copywriters who want to write clever prose, or account executives who are only interested in keeping clients happy. People with this selfish, limited view of advertising usually end up in the lower jobs, while people who force themselves to take the broad view end up on the top.
>
> *Malcolm End, Senior Vice President, Creative*
> *Director, Ogilvy & Mather*

> The best client I ever had never forgot what the advertising was supposed to do for his product. And each idea that came along was evaluated by that goal. If it fit, he said why he thought it fit. If it didn't, he tried to find a way to make it fit. He kept us focused. Everyone at the agency had enormous respect for him and they loved working with him.
>
> *An account supervisor*

> I want people entering the client side to know that *good* creative people are as dedicated to your end goal as you are. They want to sell your product . . . but also want to know that the uniqueness, the specialness of the way the advertising was written and created and art directed had something to do with that.
>
> *An art director*

2. Clearly Defined Roles

In a collaborative relationship, the individual contributor's role is as clearly defined as the organizations' roles are in the advertiser-agency contract. When roles are clearly defined, the individual becomes the expert in his area and is respected for that expertise. Contributions to his area do not pose a threat because he is recognized as the authority in his area. However, when roles are ill defined, when advertisers want to write all the copy or art directors want to change the marketing strategy, collaborators become reluctant to collaborate.

In advertising, role definition is difficult because some areas of expertise, positioning, and strategy are shared, especially by the account group, whose role is one of liaison between the advertiser and creative people.

3. Mutual Respect Based on Expertise

For any collaboration to be successful, the contributors involved must earn the respect of the other contributors by exhibiting expertise in their areas. Perhaps because advertising itself is not always respected, agency people often find it difficult to earn their client's respect, but your respect is important, especially to the creative people, if you want them to produce great advertising. Senior advertisers have learned the importance of respect.

> I'm in awe of people who can fill blank paper. They have a special gift. Some are more gifted than others, of course, but I don't ever want to crush that gift. A client must create an environment that allows them to expand. Give them the feeling that their work is important. It all comes down to a question of respect for somebody's talent.
>
> *Richard Rosenbloom, Vice President, Advertising,*
> *Card Division, American Express*

> A great source of satisfaction is the interaction with a really good creative mind. . . . Be sure you are working with the best people available because they have an important role to play in the success of your enterprise. . . . Once you're sure of that, you ought to operate as if they were truly capable of coming up with better answers than you are. It means giving them the information they need to do their job and listening to their perspective, because they have a piece of the puzzle you don't have. Together you're going to come up with a better answer than either of you could separately. But to do that, you have to respect them and treat them in a way that lets them know you're counting on their help.
>
> *Victor Elkind, Manager of Development,*
> *Main Meal Division, General Foods*

It is important that the agency respect you, too. Your business expertise, your knowledge of your own and competitive products or services will all make the agency more receptive to your contributions.

4. Mutual Trust

In any relationship, trust takes time, but entering the collaborative relationship with a commitment to trusting unless proven wrong can make the collaborative process move smoothly from the start. Mutual trust in the development of advertising means trusting the other collaborators to focus on the common goal rather than on personal goals.

> The most important elements in any strong, lasting business relationship are trust (they're on the same side working together toward the same goal), and respect (that the principles governing everyone's actions are founded in good business judgment, not emotion or internal politics).
>
> *A group product manager, health care*

5. Relaxation of Authority

In Chapter 1, it was pointed out that advertisers at the product manager level or below have a great deal of responsibility for the advertising created by their agency, but little authority over their agency. That is a major reason why the relationship with your agency is so important. Nevertheless, within the collaborative relationship, you alone must decide when the advertising is ready to show to your management. Although you and the agency are responsible for the end result, you are more responsible because the advertising is for *your* product or service; it's funded from *your* advertising budget; it affects *your* bottom line; and it is being presented to *your* bosses.

In the collaborative relationship, you are in a difficult position because you are an equal collaborator who, in the final analysis, must judge the advertising, approve it for presentation, and defend it to your management. Finding the balance between relaxation of authority and maintaining control isn't an easy task, but it is crucial to the development of outstanding advertising. According to William Weilbacher in his book *Auditing Productivity,* "The creative process and the creative work which it generates are not always amenable to highly structured organizations with clear avenues of responsibility and communication. Creativity seems to produce its greatest yields in an atmosphere that is, within reason, permissive rather than authoritarian, positively interactive rather than highly structured."[2]

Booz • Allen & Hamilton concurs: "It is up to advertiser management to provide the environment that encourages wide collaboration on an unrestrictive basis, but at the same time not lose control in the complexity of relationships that result."[3]

6. Contributing in Other Areas

In a successful collaboration built on mutual trust and respect, collaborators feel free to propose ideas in areas other than their own. Advertisers have copy ideas. Creative people suggest media. They are not afraid of making a stupid comment or of stepping on each other's toes.

> The idea of singling out the so-called "creative people" and branding them as "creative" has always struck me as being absolute elitism nonsense. Everyone helps along the way.
>
> *Bernard Rosner, Vice President, Creative Director,*
> *Ogilvy & Mather Partners*

Perhaps the following quotation best describes the feelings inherent in a successful collaborative relationship. Malcolm End, a senior vice president, creative director at Ogilvy & Mather, described his relationship with one of his clients, a director of marketing. "Trust developed quickly based on team spirit. I always felt I could enter into any discussion, or critique work in his area. As a result, I actively solicited his opinion of *my* work. On a shoot, for example, he would never say, 'Move aside, guys. Let me look in that camera.' So I'd find myself walking over to where he stood to say 'Hey, Bill . . . I think this is ready, and I think this is right. Tell me what *you* think.' It was that kind of team spirit. That absolute trust between two human beings—I don't know if it's rare, but it's not common."

When a collaborative relationship works well, it can be one of the greatest satisfactions in the marketing and advertising businesses.

> Advertising's great because it's creative and tangible. The process is a dynamic one . . . it doesn't matter if it's full of struggle because there's a camaraderie that builds up under pressure, and you both have a sense of accomplishment when it's finished.
>
> *Abby Kohnstamm, Director of Industry Marketing,*
> *American Express*

> There is nothing more exciting or enjoyable in the agency business than working with a terrific client who isn't afraid to let you contribute to his business, who really trusts you. Sure, we all work for money, but it's the satisfaction of accomplishing with someone else or a team of people that makes it all worthwhile.
>
> *An account supervisor*

> I've had very rewarding agency relationships. . . . I'd like to think that some of that is my responsibility.
>
> *A product manager, cigarettes*

A successful collaboration can be achieved, but far too often the collaborative relationship is elusive. Before setting out some guidelines for you to follow to achieve and maintain the collaboration, you should be aware of the attitudes collaborators bring to the relationship that usually hinder its chances for success.

ATTITUDES THAT POISON A SUCCESSFUL COLLABORATION

Ultimately, *you* are responsible for the advertising you get from your agency. Even though agency creative and account people bring many attitudes to the advertiser-agency collaboration that hinder its success, the most potentially destructive attitudes are brought into the relationship by the advertisers, because they control the purse strings.

THE SIX ADVERTISER POISONS

"I'm the boss here!" Although advertisers do judge the agency's work and must be responsible for it, flaunting that power—using position to get one's way even if it hurts the advertising results—poisons the agency's desire to generate great advertising. This is an attitude that is regrettably too pervasive among advertisers. The following quotations are anonymous for obvious reasons and do not bode well for a healthy partnership.

> I'll be honest with you. I switched from the agency to the client side because that's where the power is.
>
> *A product manager, health and beauty aids*

> I tell the account people that this is how I do business. I say, "As far as I'm concerned we're in this together, guys, and as much as I respect the relationship, I'm the client and you're going to basically serve me. Right? Right!"
>
> *A group product manager, health and beauty aids*

> I love agency people. The problem is I don't know how much to tip them.
>
> *A marketing manager, food*

> Sometimes I wish the agency in a secure client-agency relationship wouldn't feel so secure.
>
> *A product manager, financial services*

> We're the client. We don't have to put up with this.
>
> *A product manager, food*

> I think that managing an agency well is just like bringing up children, like getting the best out of children. And managing a client well is recognizing that they're in the parental role . . . the child can get the best direction, best praise or punishment, best rewards, recognition, and the parents can get the best pictures.
>
> *A general manager, food*

> I once worked with a junior client. He'd been in the business only a year, out of business school for two years. He wanted to put an important word in a print ad headline in red so it would stand out. I explained all the reasons why this would hurt the advertise-

ment, all I'd learned in my ten-plus years in advertising, and at
the end of the explanation he paused and then said, "Well, I'm not
convinced." The words I should have heard from this young up-
start were, "Thank you for taking the time to explain it to me."

A vice president, account supervisor

These attitudes are counterproductive to the creation of superior
advertising, as they make agency people feel that their ideas
will not be used no matter how beneficial they are.

Tracy Kelly, product manager at Bristol-Myers, best sum-
marized the first advertiser poison: "The single biggest mistake
that clients make is not to really believe that the agency is a
partner—a business partner. And if they espouse that philosophy at all, they seem to only give it lip service. . . . Most client
people want to be important, and that can be difficult for clients
to pull off when they work in megastructures. One of the ways to
feel important is to push some vendor around. And oftentimes
agencies fall within the definition of vendor. So giving lip service to having the agency be a business partner is a way of
behaving like you're working with them the way you should, but
all the time really wanting to maintain control over them."

"My management will never buy it." Few things cause
more disrespect, lack of trust, and frustration among agency
people than a client's refusal to support and develop a good idea
because he's afraid his superiors won't like it. Although agency
people understand your position of responsibility and vul-
nerability, they also believe that they are working together with
you—collaborating—to create the best possible way to sell your
product or service. If the idea is good, and you believe it, you
cannot let second-guessing your boss kill it. That's how outstanding advertising becomes mediocre advertising. The agency
will aid your courage by helping you develop arguments to
convince those in power, but if you are afraid to make a decision,
you surely will defeat your agency's drive to create great
advertising, too.

"I'm a better person than you are." For some reason,
many, many advertisers embrace the notion that they are supe-

rior to the people they work with at the agency. Perhaps the attitude arises because they deal with tangible products or professional services and the agency people are in the elusive "show business" of advertising. Whatever the reason, it's a problem that can hurt the mutual respect and trust necessary to create outstanding advertising.

> The problem is bigger than just power, I think. My vantage point is limited to large packaged goods companies and large agencies. We tend to recruit from the same places, the same business schools, and we get the same kinds of people. But for reasons I'm not really sure I can understand, those in the class who become clients immediately start looking down at those in their class who go to agencies. They tend to feel that what the agency account people are doing isn't as important or as meaningful or as challenging as what they're doing. . . . I try to remind them that it wasn't that many months ago that they were in the same class with a lot of these people. And what brought these people to the agency is not necessarily that they couldn't get a job with the client, because a lot didn't *want* a job with the client—agency talents are every bit as worthy of respect as client ones. . . . So you have not only this power trip, "you do what I tell you to do or else," you have this feeling of intellectual and job superiority. It's a serious problem.
>
> *A general manager, food*

"What if their idea is better than mine?"   This is the poison of fear. It takes a secure individual to realize that another person's idea is better than his own, accept that idea, and use it to further his goals and not view it as a professional threat.

> It becomes difficult to be a hotshot yourself if the agency is a true business partner and is coming up with ideas that are potentially better than yours. The insecure client doesn't see this as making him or her look good. The insecure client will see this as competition.
>
> *Tracy Kelly, Product Manager, Bristol-Myers*

Any manager of any group of people has to learn to let those who are helping him shine, and understand that the shine reflects back on himself. A sales success helps everyone associated with it, and it takes as much talent and brains to recognize a good idea as it does to create one.

Withholding information. One clever but nonetheless self-defeating way advertisers make certain that the agency never comes up with a better idea than they do is to withhold information needed to create advertising or develop a point of view on a marketing problem.

> Information is power. If they are given too much, it becomes more and more difficult to maintain control over them.
>
> *A product manager, health and beauty aids*

Thus, by withholding information, some advertisers maintain their power position, but it is the most destructive way to lower the effectiveness of advertising.

Fear of the creative people. Too many advertisers distance themselves from the creative people because they find it hard to relate to a style of dress or a style of life different from their own. They may even fear creative people and think the creative process is somehow magical.

> Some managers just cannot relate to the creative people. Sometimes they don't even approach them as human beings. They're these strange people they don't know how to talk to. They have weird points of view. They dress strangely.
>
> *Mary Seggerman, Senior Product Manager, General Foods*

> Clients that wish they were creatives and don't become them think, "Gee, I'm not crazy enough to do that."
>
> *Jeff Atlas, Copywriter, Ogilvy & Mather*

Of course, we are describing a stereotype. Not all creative people wear "strange" clothing or follow bizarre lifestyles. Those that do are often encouraged by agencies and advertisers to look the part. In fact, some creative people dress creatively to help sell their ideas!

To relate to creative people more easily, you might consider following a suggestion of Ronald Leong, group product manager, Bristol-Myers: "What better way to learn about advertising than to actually write advertisements . . . you understand how difficult it is, how much easier the job of the creative person is when one can clearly communicate, focus the problem in his terms."

THE FOUR ADVERTISING-ACCOUNT-GROUP POISONS

Dishonesty.   Dishonesty by account people doesn't appear because those people lie or lack ethical or moral standards. Rather, it most often surfaces because the account person is trying to embrace differing points of view (the advertiser's or the agency's) and espouse them even if they differ from what she truly believes. It can take two forms. The first is agreeing with the advertiser's point of view simply to make him happy. She may believe his ideas will not help build his sales, but rather than presenting a convincing argument based on the agency's expertise, she tells him that he is right. Agreeing with him is easier, and a happy client is far less likely to cause problems for the agency. However, the point she is missing is that his happiness will fade when the advertising fails to produce results.

The second form dishonesty can take is trying to convince an advertiser to run advertising that focuses more on the agency's creativity than on selling his product or service. The agency's goal is showcase advertising to attract new business, and she has put aside the common goal of success in the marketplace.

Dishonesty is unattractive, frustrating. Most important, it poisons the trust and respect you must have to collaborate with your agency people to produce highly effective advertising of which both advertiser and agency can feel proud.

"I'm a better person than you are."   As many advertisers believe they are superior to agency people because their job is more meaningful and challenging, so, too, many agency people believe they are superior because their job is creative and glamorous. In fact, some think people on the advertiser side are dull and boring and lead dull, boring lives.

Well, look at them. They all wear three-piece suits. Even the women. They all live in the suburbs, have 2.3 children, and joining the country club is their only life's goal. I'm exaggerating, of course, but they work with numbers and finance and manufacturing all day. I couldn't do their job. I'd be bored out of my mind.

An account supervisor

Failure to listen.   Many advertisers interviewed for this book mentioned failure to listen as their greatest frustration with agency people, because when agencies fail to listen to client direction, work that may take them months to create is off target and often unusable. One reason agency people may not always listen well is their inclination to start solving the advertising problem before it has been completely defined. Once a solution is reached, they sometimes don't want to hear the rest of the facts because they may have to discard the solution they have already created and go "back to the drawing board." Advertisers can fail to listen, too, but the agency's failure to listen is potentially more of a problem because it is the agency that executes the advertising.

"We create the advertising, not you."   Some agency people are extremely jealous of their role as creators of the advertising and are hesitant to let their clients contribute. This "not invented here" attitude is the antithesis of collaboration. Advertisers who present their ideas as suggestions, rather than dictate from their position of power, should expect fair consideration of their ideas. Good agency people know that good clients can make the advertising better.

THE TWO CREATIVE POISONS

Creativity for its own sake.   Whenever art directors or copywriters create visuals or words that do not contribute to the overall effectiveness of the advertising, they are poisoning the collaborative relationship. However, it sometimes happens because creative people want unusual, highly creative advertising in their portfolios, because they want to win awards, and because their agency management may want unusual, highly creative advertising on its new business reel.

What can a client do about it? Challenge your creative people to defend their ideas. Try to remember that creating fresh approaches to the advertising problem is the creative people's job and that it's better to err on the highly creative side than on the ordinary side. Finally, try to trust and remember that true professionals always have success in the marketplace as their primary goal.

"I'm a better person than you are."   Giving criticism to creative people is a skill that takes practice. However, receiving criticism is also a skill, and some creative people are very bad at it. They are difficult to collaborate with—for both advertisers and agency account people. They feel that they are more creative, interesting people—they are the writers and art directors and, therefore, the only people who know anything about creating advertising. They refuse to listen to ideas; they look down their creative noses at you; they act superior and even *arrogant.*

Unfortunately, some creative people have these attitudes but at the same time produce outstanding work. You may obtain a superior end result, but have a far more difficult time getting there.

THE COMMON POISONS

Two attitudes are the most poisonous to a collaborative relationship because they are brought by all collaborators: first, placing a personal goal—whether it be power, appeasement, or creativity for its own sake—ahead of the common goal; second, feeling superior to the other collaborators. Obviously, you can't control the attitudes of your agency people (it may be difficult enough controlling those that are yours). However, being aware of and understanding that all collaborators have common destructive attitudes as well as a common goal can help you create a successful collaboration and obtain the fruits of that collaboration: advertising that is a success in the marketplace.

The next chapter will focus on the most effective general management skills and how they apply to working with your agency.

NOTES—CHAPTER 4

1. Booz • Allen & Hamilton, Inc., *Management & Advertising Problems in the Advertiser-Agency Relationship* (New York: Association of National Advertisers, Inc., 1965), p. 113.
2. William M. Weilbacher, *Auditing Productivity* (New York: Association of National Advertisers, Inc., 1981), p. 14.
3. Booz • Allen & Hamilton, Inc., *op. cit.*, p. 117.

CASE 6.
The Complacent Copy Contact

YOU ARE: A copywriter with account executive responsibilities on one small account that occupies about 20 percent of your time. You are the major agency contact on the business and report directly to the president of the agency, who has delegated most of his responsibilities to you, including reviewing the advertising before presentation to the client. You have run the account and worked with the client's advertising director for over five years.

THE PROBLEM: Recently, a once-strong relationship with the advertising director has become tense and strained. Copy criticisms have increased and are given in anger. Requests for work are given unrealistically fast due dates. When you questioned the timing of his latest request, the advertising director asked you, "Does your agency still want our business?" What should you do?

chapter 5

What it takes to get the best?

If you're now thinking, "I get it! Managing advertising is really managing people," you are right on target.

People are virtually the only variable in the creation of advertising. After all, what else is there? A few colored markers, a typewriter or word processor, and lots of blank paper. It's the combination of the talent, intelligence, and energy of the account and creative people assigned to your business plus the knowledge you give them and the excitement you are able to generate that will produce the best advertising product for you.

> The advertiser-agency relationship is the most important thing in the whole business. Today fewer and fewer relationships are being built because advertisers are too busy to take the time. That's foolish. If they invest the time with their agency people, they will get back triple the effort. Relationships are what make this business work.
>
> *G. F. "Pete" Tyrrell, Vice President, Advertising,*
> *Corporate Staff, Johnson & Johnson*

Advertisers who throughout their careers are able to build the best agency relationships and get the best work have eight characteristics in common, eight basic management principles that they adopt to the special nature of the advertiser-agency relationship.

Incidentally, these eight characteristics also happen to form the definition of what agency people call a "good client," but that's not a good reason to start practicing them. A good reason is that they work. They get the best advertising from your agency.

Advertisers who are most effective with their agencies . . .

DELEGATE

They let the agency do its job.

You let your accountant do his job, your lawyer do her job; yet, when it comes to writing advertising, everyone wants to get into the act. Because we're all exposed to so much advertising, we all think we can create it. Writing advertising looks easy enough, and it is easy . . . to write a bad ad.

However, creating an ad that can really build your business takes talent, training, technique, and discipline—years of it— and the chances of a professional advertising person coming up with a big idea are far greater than you coming up with one.

Additionally, if you delegate to your agency, you give them the responsibility for your advertising. That creates more involvement and commitment.

> Since a corporation hires an agency to do its creative work, it's necessary to delegate so the agency has the responsibility to act on your behalf. You can't hold the agency accountable if you do their job. If the ads don't work, you have no one to blame but yourself. You'd have to fire yourself. . . . Large agencies got large because they're experts at creating good advertising. It's when clients get in the way of the creative process that advertising starts to suffer. Bad advertising is almost always the failure of the client, not the agency.
>
> *Edward C. MacEwen, Vice President, Corporate Communications, GTE Corporation*

> Over the years I found that many of my colleagues tend to view the agency as a support group that you dictate to. Do this. Do that. Ultimately you get mediocre to good advertising, rarely great advertising. You get what you ask for and nothing else.
>
> *Ray Abrahamsen, Director of Marketing, Church & Dwight*

> To get the best work from an agency, I think it's critically important to establish an atmosphere of confidence in them. A good agency feels very strongly about your business and has strongly felt ideas on how to build that business. A good client lets them know that their feelings count and is willing to back the agency's ideas, at least to try them. But be sure you follow through. If you say you're going to try some advertising the agency is interested in, do it and see how it works. Don't put them

through numerous storyboard iterations and then bail out on the idea before making a commercial.

Stephen W. Rutledge, Vice President, Advertising, Kraft, Inc.

Delegating to the agency does not mean that you can't have ideas about the advertising—far from it. But hang on to your ideas; tuck them away in the back of your mind until the agency can show you what they've created. Give them the full responsibility for the assignment. If their ideas aren't as good as or better than yours, then share your ideas with them. You may lose a few weeks, but you'll have vastly increased their enthusiasm and commitment to doing their best work for you.

GIVE CLEAR, CONSISTENT DIRECTION

Get your act together before you pick up the phone. That includes clearing your direction with your management. Let the agency know how you need them to help build your business, what specifically you want them to do, and by when. Try not to change direction in the middle of an assignment. Nothing saps enthusiasm more than having to go back and start all over again after a job is half-completed.

The worst thing that can happen to the agency is to get a new set of ground-rules at each step through the client's approval system. Brand management and agency should work together to articulate creative objectives and strategies. Then brand management should make certain there is internal client awareness of, and agreement to, the goals. The agency will then have a clear sense of direction and, at the approval stage, discussion can be focused on the specific advertising being presented.

Robert K. Powell, Director of Advertising, Kraft, Inc.

If you are in a fast-changing business, such as those in high technology, the business itself may force you to change direction to the agency. If you warn your agency people about this possibility in advance, if you explain this in your agency briefing (see Chapter 8), they will be far better able to accept the change. Change actually becomes a part of the business problem.

GIVE GOOD INFORMATION

In order to create advertising for your business, your agency must understand your business. The more you share with them, the better your chances of getting advertising that meets your needs.

> Take the agency in as an equal partner in the marketing process. Manifest that by not being a barrier to them in getting the information they need. Good communications people are not threatened when the agency meets with internal people because they know it leads to the best advertising. Let the agency interface with whomever they need to.
>
> *Robert E. Williams, Managing Director of Marketing*
> *Communications, E. I. du Pont de Nemours & Company*

> The more you can tell your agency about your business, the more involved they will feel. An agency can't work in the dark. If they don't know the facts about your business, they can easily do work that is off strategy. That wastes your time and money. Clients that share their business problems get better work.
>
> *Thomas Watson, President, Diversified Agency Services,*
> *Division of Omnicom Group, Inc.*

> An agency can be an intimate advisor to both the advertising and non-advertising parts of your business. They can bring a fresh, unbiased point of view. You need to feed them information—and sometimes force-feed them, if they're reluctant to go beyond just advertising—so that they understand how to help.
>
> *Brian Ruder, Director of Marketing, Pepsi-Cola U.S.A.*

> Better clients give you all the information that you need to know and then some to go about your job. They're willing to spend some money on research if there are some unanswered questions; they don't guess at answers; they're not lazy. Some kinds of assignments require that the clients give you more information and when you go back and say "I need this," lots of clients will rebel, and it's because it's extra work for them. The good clients are ones that will go the extra step with you."
>
> *Sy Waldman, Lockwood & Waldman Advertising, Inc.*

Giving good information not only makes the agency a part of your business but also it provides the stimulus for the creation of your advertising; therefore, don't ever be afraid of giving too much information. But don't forget to organize it.

ARE OPEN-MINDED

Being open-minded to the advertising presented to you doesn't mean you can't have an idea yourself. (How can you not have an idea when you are shaping an assignment for the agency!) Being open-minded means evaluating the advertising your agency presents on its own merit: Does it communicate the key benefit? Is it on strategy? Is it executed well?—not on whether it meets your preconceived idea of what the ad would be. You should want the agency to create the best advertising for your business, not read your mind.

> Too much timidity up front could have robbed IBM of a multi-million dollar big idea. And I think any advertising manager must be careful not to reject out-of-hand an advertising idea that he or she thinks is certain not to get clearance by the company management, network broadcast standards departments, or whatever.
>
> In developing advertising for IBM's personal computer, the agency, Lord, Geller, Federico, Einstein, Inc., wanted to use the famous Charlie Chaplin Little Tramp character as a symbol for Everyman. They reasoned that the character was well known, and would disarm many people's fear of computers.
>
> If one wanted to look for drawbacks to using the character, it wasn't hard to think of a lot of them right away. First of all, Charlie Chaplin had been a controversial figure in the United States. Second, one of Chaplin's most famous movies, *Modern Times,* depicted the Little Tramp character as being dehumanized by modern technology. Third, his Tramp character was marked by shabby clothes, holes in his shoes and other elements which did not seem to make him the perfect stand-in for an IBM customer.
>
> However, after some debate at several levels, the decision was made to go forward and the rest is advertising history. The Little Tramp character became famous as IBM's spokesman for personal computers around the world.
>
> *Charles G. Francis, former Corporate Director of*
> *Advertising and Promotion, IBM*

I guess the best thing I've learned is listen, listen and be open-minded. I think we all have tendencies to think that our ideas are the best ideas, that our way of thinking is the best and only way of thinking, and if you don't think the way I think, then surely your way of thinking is not good. That's something that I've had to overcome. This industry tends to draw a group of people who are smart and motivated and somewhat egotistical, and I think we all need to work at overcoming those ego problems.

Shiela Hopkins, Group Product Manager, Shulton, Inc.

What I basically want is the chance, that's the key word. If the client would only give people a chance. And when I think of the best clients to work with, they were open to doing something different. I don't mean changing the strategy. I don't mean killing a good campaign that was working. I mean just open to doing something different. A fresh idea.

An associate creative director

A client owes the agency the right to try an occasional idea the agency believes in even if the client doesn't. Conversely, the agency owes the client the absolutely most inspired copy on an idea the client believes in but the agency doesn't.

Joel D. Weiner, Senior Vice President, Corporate
Marketing, Kraft, Inc.

SHOW APPRECIATION

Few people work only for their paychecks. They work for a lot more, including satisfaction, recognition, and appreciation for a job well done. Showing that appreciation is even more important for agency creative people because of the personal, human element they must put into the advertising to make it effective.

Therefore, when an assignment is very well done, send a thank-you note to your creative people. An occasional thank-you note will rededicate and reenergize your whole agency team.

Many years ago, we found ourselves thrust into big-time network television in the form of a three-hour special. The program was going to air in three months, and we didn't have a single commercial on the shelf. With luck and a seven-day workweek, both at IBM and the agency, we managed to meet the deadline. The Corporate Vice President of Communications at the time set up a luncheon in our executive dining room for everyone in the agency who had worked on the project. She told them how much their work had meant to the company. The effect on the agency people is hard to describe. They couldn't get over it and talked about the event for many years.

We learned a lesson from this and now host a breakfast for our agency every Christmas. We use the occasion to say thanks, and the agency puts on various skits and spoofs of IBM advertising management. It has become an annual tradition which has built an extraordinary client-agency relationship.

Charles G. Francis, former Corporate Director of
Advertising and Promotion, IBM

I could remember when I was new in the business and coming out of a copy meeting where we had seen some really good copy. The product manager at the time sat down and said, "We should really write them a thank-you note." I thought, "That's strange." But he did it, and I can remember the next time we saw the creative guys, they were ecstatic. I mean they were so thrilled that someone had taken the time to say, "That was a good job; keep up the good work."

Shiela Hopkins, Group Product Manager, Shulton, Inc.

SHOW RESPECT

Respect is a word that is so easy to say and so hard to make happen. It must be earned by both sides. Respect is a crucial building block of the collaborative relationship.

You must respect each other's roles if you're going to make the relationship work.

Robert E. Williams, Managing Director of Marketing
Communications, E. I. du Pont de Nemours & Company

We look for a loyal and trusting relationship with our agencies so we can share confidential data and have the same vision.

Joel D. Weiner, Senior Vice President,
Corporate Marketing, Kraft, Inc.

The presence of respect alone won't turn your agency people on, although it's an important beginning. However, its absence will surely turn them off.

There's an enormous amount of paranoia among some advertisers. People are convinced that the agency is out to dupe them.
Maybe because they think advertising does the same thing. This
causes hostility on the agency side. It makes people get into their
trenches. You never get anywhere near the talent. To get great
advertising you need to be a team and pool resources. That's the
most important thing.

Connie Sartain, Vice President, Public Affairs,
The Prudential Insurance Company of America

One manager I used to work with would clearly verbalize his lack
of respect for the agency people. He would ask their opinion and
then quickly turn around as if to say, "Your thoughts on this
subject are totally meaningless. I'm asking only because I'm
supposed to." It became clear a few weeks into the relationship
the agency was literally so unenthusiastic and so unmotivated
that we weren't getting their best work. And they felt that they
had no desire to provide their best work because, regardless of
what they did, this guy would simply turn around and do exactly
what he wanted to do. As a result, everyone got less than what
they could have gotten. The agency was unhappy, unmotivated,
felt unrespected, and the client wasn't getting good work.

Group product manager, cosmetics

SET HIGH STANDARDS

The Salz Survey of Advertiser-Agency Relations (see Appendix),
conducted among the top 200 advertisers and top 100 agencies,
found that advertisers who set high standards for their agency's
work were far more likely to get great advertising than those
who didn't.

Setting high standards means both wanting outstanding
advertising and being open to new types of executions, taking
creative risks.

It's important to understand that creativity, by definition,
involves doing at least some things differently. When you're on
the bottom rungs of the ladder, it's natural to want to do things
the right way, which, in some companies, means the way they've
always been done. But in advertising, if you just do things the

way they've always been done, you get advertising that's either just like what you've been running or just like your competition's. That isn't the best route to creating a unique positioning for your product or service.

However, wanting outstanding advertising isn't enough. To set high standards, you need to tell your agency that you expect outstanding work, and you need to consistently approve their best work.

> We've trained the agency to think big by what we've done. We've run a lot of unusual advertising. We want them to think big, think new, think different. But it's something you have to prove. You can say it, but if you don't do it, they'll stop thinking big.
>
> *Brian Ruder, Director of Marketing, Pepsi-Cola U.S.A.*

> If you know a client really wants something that's breakthrough, and by that I don't mean weird. I mean effective advertising, but fresh, effective advertising. If you know a client really wants that, it is much easier for you to break your boundaries so you can get fresher ideas. I try to do that for all clients, because what's important to me, whether the client knows they've got it or not, is to do work that I think is fresh, different and will really sell the product. It's easier for me to do that when I've got clients who want that kind of work from me and who appreciate it.
>
> *Kathleen Cantwell, Creative and Marketing Consultant*

FORM A COLLABORATIVE TEAM

If you are able to delegate to your agency, give clear, consistent direction, give good information, be open-minded, show appreciation and respect, and set high standards, you will be well on your way to getting good advertising. However, to get the best, you must go one giant step further and apply these skills to the development and maintenance of a strong, collaborative relationship. That relationship is so important, it is the subject of the rest of this book. We'll begin before you even have met your agency and finish only when the advertising is ready to be released to the media.

CASE 7.
The Correct and Only Priority

YOU ARE: An advertising manager.
THE PROBLEM: Your business has been declining for about six months. Your analysis, as well as that of your marketing people, indicates that while other factors may be contributing, the advertising doesn't appear to be working as hard as it should. You have asked the agency, through your account executive, to explore alternate copy approaches. The account executive has responded that the agency doesn't like business results to dictate their actions.
　　What should you do?

CASE 8.
Twenty Questions

YOU ARE: An assistant advertising manager at a high-technology company.
THE PROBLEM: You have learned in the year or so that you have been on the job that no matter how thoroughly you brief the agency, they always have additional questions for which you must search for answers. You are frankly tired of bothering your technical people to obtain what often seem like meaningless facts or statistics.
　　What should you do about this situation?

CASE 9.
Timing Is Everything

YOU ARE: A product manager.
THE PROBLEM: You and the agency have just agreed to a new creative strategy for your product. The agency is about to begin a creative exploratory of new campaigns. In the course of the strategy development, you have thought of what you think is a great advertising idea and you are anxious to share it with the agency. In fact, you'd like to see them execute it along with their own ideas as part of their first presentation to you.
　　Should you tell them your idea now? Why or why not?

chapter 6

The collaborative relationship: Seven steps to establish it

During your marketing career, you will develop many new relationships with the people at an advertising agency. Your company may hire a new agency; new agency people may be assigned to your account; you may change jobs within your current company or move to a new company and, therefore, work with new agency people. In any of these situations there is a beginning and thereby an opportunity to establish the relationship that produces the best advertising—the collaborative relationship.

As the advertiser, you should take the responsibility for setting the tone of the relationship with your agency people and for creating the environment that fosters collaboration. It is for you and your company that the agency is working. Although you may have limited authority over the agency, you are nevertheless the leader. Of course, the agency is also responsible for their relationships with their clients. (One of the account group's main tasks is simply to get along with the client. Agency account people are evaluated by their management on their ability to work well with many different people.) However, because you are the client, the agency will willingly or unwillingly follow your lead in developing the type of relationship you want. Since a collaborative relationship will produce the best advertising, that is the relationship you should strive to achieve with your agency. The following seven steps will help you establish it.

SET THE STANDARDS FOR GREAT ADVERTISING

This is an obvious step that almost everyone overlooks. Simply tell your agency account and creative people that you want and expect effective advertising of which you will all be proud, and that you will do everything you can to help them create it. Tell them that any idea, no matter how unusual, is worthy of consideration, and they should never be afraid to show it to you.

Every person at the agency wants nothing more than a real opportunity to do what he does best, and a client who tells him he is being given that opportunity, and means it, will set the stage for the creation of truly outstanding advertising.

> Do whatever you can to convince the agency that you want great advertising and that you'll treat them and what they do with respect and love.
>
> *A general manager, food*

INITIATE TWO-WAY COMMUNICATION

Don't be afraid to step down from your advertiser position, relax your authority, and participate in the collaboration as an equal. Of course, you are responsible to your management for the advertising and, therefore, want to exercise your limited authority so that you feel comfortable with the agency's work. However, to obtain the best advertising, you must be part of the collaborative process in which your ideas are accepted because of your expertise, not dictated from your position of authority. To create the right chemistry for collaboration, you must give the agency as much right to criticize and question your ideas as you do theirs.

> Believe that it's your responsibility to know them and work with them every bit as much as it is theirs to know and work with you. It's all part of this attitude of the agency being the vendor, of "I'll sit back and they'll call me. They should do what I want." That attitude should be avoided at all costs. . . . Take them seriously as a body of people who are there to accomplish something. Make sure that they count in your mind one hundred percent. They can help you a lot; they can also hurt you a lot. They're not there to do your bidding, to polish your shoes.
>
> *Tracy Kelly, Product Manager, Bristol-Myers*

Give them respect, information, knowledge, and instill a two-way attitude and you're going to get the best. Trust and confidence work both ways.

Richard Rosenbloom, Vice President, Advertising,
Card Division, American Express

Give them respect at the beginning. Try to develop that working relationship. Don't be afraid to let them get to know you. Try to get to know them. If they're playing games or politics, then you've got to drop back and reevaluate the situation. That's the tough part. It's tough to get honesty right at the beginning. But my feeling is the people I've met in this business are all self-motivated. They're anxious to do a good job. They're honest.

John Deford, Product Manager, Colgate

DEVELOP A PERSONAL RELATIONSHIP WITH YOUR AGENCY PEOPLE

It is virtually impossible to collaborate on a purely professional level, because as ideas and feelings are shared and common goals are achieved, the relationship grows more personal. You should try to encourage everyone's personal involvement, including your own, because people are more productive if they are valued for who they are as well as for the work they produce. This is a basic management rule.

The creative process also involves personal risks in the form of rejection of ideas. In a collaborative relationship where all participants are contributing, they need to trust in order to tell each other the unusual creative ideas that can lead to outstanding advertising ideas. The more personal the relationship, the more trust can exist.

Another reason for developing personal relationships is that the creative people are personally involved in their advertising product; they have to be in order to create advertising that communicates on a personal level with consumers. They are taking the biggest personal risk of all collaborators and, therefore, benefit most from the support of a good personal relationship with the advertiser. The better you know your creative people, the more you can help them to take those risks.

I think one of the important keys to good advertising is to be able to develop a good working and personal relationship with all the people involved in the business, whether they be account people or creative people.

Ronald Leong, Group Product Manager, Bristol-Myers

My advice to a new assistant product manager is to get to know the agency account personnel personally. Know them and know how they think.

An assistant product manager, cigarettes

I don't just like getting to know my brand people, I *want* to get to know them. My job is to help them build their business. And since that leads to their business success, that leads to their personal success as well. If they care about succeeding, then I want to care, too. It gives me personal satisfaction to help someone, and I guess that's one of the reasons I'm a good account supervisor.

A vice president, account supervisor

Within the subject of personal relationships, there are two controversial areas we ought to review: the role of socializing and advertiser contact with creative people. The advertising business is both famous and infamous for the amount of socializing that occurs. Although the three-martini lunch is now a rarity, advertisers and agencies socialize because of the importance of forming personal relationships. Lunch, dinner, or an afterwork drink offer the ideal environment for stripping off business veneers and discussing common problems more openly.

However, you should beware of the seduction of agency people and agency socializing. Agency people want you to be happy. One way to do that is to make you feel important. They always remember your birthday, your favorite restaurant, and your favorite type of food, but unless you have truly become good personal friends with your agency counterparts, next year, when you're no longer on the business, more than likely they will have forgotten your birthday. Use the socializing offered to further the personal relationships with the objective of producing better advertising, but also try to remember that you are being entertained because of the position you hold as well as your personality.

The second controversial area of personal relationships is

advertiser contact with creative people. Many agencies believe that advertisers should have only limited contact with their creative people—meetings, an occasional lunch, but no direct phone calls or requests. They believe creative people should have only one boss: the creative director. Even though the advertising is being developed for your business, it must first live up to the agency's standards and be judged by people whose primary expertise is advertising. They also believe creative people must focus solely on the advertising problem presented to them in the form of the creative strategy. Once creative people have begun the creative process, input from other people, advertisers, or account group is confusing rather than helpful.

Nevertheless, too much distance from creative people hinders the free exchange of ideas. If contact is limited only to formal meetings, the collaborative process suffers. The happy medium would be to socialize with the creative people after meetings, while respecting their reporting lines and necessary creative isolation.

> Writers and people who do the work never get to be with or talk to the people they're doing the work for. There's an account group in between. Clients aren't allowed to talk to creative people. What's bad about this is that it tends to perpetuate the myth that creative people are strange individuals you can't talk to like regular people. You can't say "I think that's a dull piece of advertising" because they'll kill you, themselves, or both.
>
> *A general manager, food*

INVOLVE THE AGENCY IN YOUR BUSINESS

If you want the best advertising from your agency, involve them in your business. The more they know, the better the advertising they can create. Additionally, you should ask their opinions in all areas of your business that pertain to marketing, or as many as permitted by your company philosophy or agency contract. Involvement will make your agency people feel that their contributions are valued and that their ideas can have an effect on your business. Your goals will become their goals, and they will be motivated to contribute more than is required. They may even have some good ideas to help you solve your business's problems.

> I believe the agency should be an extension of your brand group and your activities. . . . I'm a firm believer in involving agency personnel, whether they be creative or account people, heavily into the business—not only in the process of developing advertising, but in the whole process of managing the business. If you can't create a partnership and a good working relationship with the agency, then it's going to be the kind of relationship that becomes almost adversarial. . . . I don't think that's a productive or an optimum environment for getting terrific advertising.
>
> *Ronald Leong, Group Product Manager, Bristol-Myers*

> Think of your agency as part of the organization. Then it becomes a partnership, not an adversary relationship. One of the nice things about my biggest account is they gave me a key to their office. From day one, when I went there, I went up in the elevator, then, instead of going to the receptionist, I went to a locked door. I opened the door myself and walked right into their offices. I said to myself, "That's a bloody good client-agency relationship. It presumes we're both on the same team."
>
> *Bernard Rosner, Vice President, Creative*
> *Director, Ogilvy & Mather Partners*

To involve your agency in your business, explain your company structure fully to your account group. Draw them a diagram. Include the background of key company personnel. Next, explain all facets of your job to them, including the current problems you may be facing in manufacturing, sales, and other areas with which they are not intimately involved. They will then understand your business and how their function, advertising, fits into your overall responsibilities. Your explanation could include a tour of your offices or your factory, with introductions to the key personnel in manufacturing, sales, R&D. On a regular basis, tell your agency about sales achievements, company personnel changes, manufacturing or distribution problems. Finally, talk to them informally about a marketing problem you may be struggling with. Use the agency as a sounding board. Again, they may have some good ideas about your business, just as you may have some good ideas about advertising.

Some clients are reluctant to involve agency people in their business because it appears to have no immediate effect on moving their business ahead, because agency people may move to another job and take company secrets with them, and because agency personnel, especially at the account executive level, change every year or so and briefing must be repeated. However, none of the above reasons is as important as the difference in the amount and quality of work from agency people who are involved compared to those who are excluded from their client's business. Incidentally, a good account person will try to become involved in your business even if you are reluctant to involve him. He will continually ask you questions about all aspects of your business.

LEARN ALL YOU CAN ABOUT THE AGENCY

Learn about their structure: who reports to whom; who the agency's other clients are and what they bill; where your company fits in; which agency people have to see and approve copy before you see it. Learn about their philosophy of advertising, the rules they might have that guide them in creating outstanding advertising. Learn whether they are dominated by the creative department or account management. The answer can determine both the freshness of the advertising and the level of frustration in the creative process. In the most *extreme* examples, an account-dominated agency has more of a tendency to see the advertiser's perspective, to focus most on the effectiveness of the advertising rather than on the freshness and uniqueness of the advertising executions. In a creative-dominated agency, efforts are focused on preserving the freshness of the executions as well as the effectiveness. Advertiser's changes that sacrifice freshness for effectiveness are resisted far more strongly.

> Take a little time to get to know the people, what they're like, how they work. Spend a little time asking them what their line of command is and how their work is handled in terms of who has to see it. . . . If you understand what constraints they're working

under and vice versa, you have a better chance of getting productive things out of each other.

Tamar Bernbaum, Associate Product Manager, Colgate

To learn about your agency, ask to review their new-business reel. It includes the advertising the agency considers its best. The reel will not only show you the calibre of work the agency is capable of creating, it will also show you the kind of work they prefer to do. If there aren't any commercials for your product or service on the reel, find out why they're not proud enough of the advertising to show it to prospective clients.

USE THE AGENCY'S KNOWLEDGE OF YOUR BUSINESS

If the agency has been working on your product or service and you're new, the agency can be invaluable in helping you learn your business. You can ask them questions you might be embarrassed to ask your boss or colleagues.

Ask the agency as many questions as possible. This way you get the benefit of their knowledge and it also shows them that you care about how they feel about the business.

Tracy Kelly, Product Manager, Bristol-Myers

Listen as much as you can. Try to learn what works and what doesn't from what you observe.

Abby Kohnstamm, Director of Industry Marketing, American Express

When I first got on the business I felt dependent on the agency to help me learn. . . . I learned to question everything. Does it make sense? If you have a question about something, ask it. Approach the agency with "I'm new at this. You're the person I'm going to learn from. I'm going to ask a lot of questions." So that way, you really are learning. You're forcing the agency to think twice about what they're doing, and you're letting them know that they're not going to be able to put something over on you because you're going to be asking about it.

Ellen Elias, Group Product Manager, Lever Brothers

MAKE YOUR FIRST AGENCY MEETING A COLLABORATION

Starting off on the right foot with your agency is crucial, but not difficult. In one meeting you can set the tone for your long-term working relationship, motivate the agency, learn how they think, see the kind of work they do, and learn about your business. If you're new to the business, simply ask your account executive to prepare and present a review of competitive copy and your brand's copy with both the account and creative groups present. Follow the presentation with an agency tour and lunch.

In just a few hours, you and the agency will accomplish a lot together. You will exchange views about advertising. Because you are all reviewing competitors' advertising, created by neither the agency nor your predecessor, you can all comment without defenses or vested interest. You will learn part of your business—your competitors' position in the marketplace and how advertising helped or hurt them.

During the competitive review you can also ask questions about advertising for your own business in relation to competitive advertising. Questioning in this context may be less threatening to the agency. Ask them to be as objective as possible about it. Did the advertising turn out the way they wanted? What changes were made in the advertising after it was originally presented? By whom? Be careful to make your comments about the agency's advertising as positive and general as possible. Don't judge. At the first meeting you have much to lose and little to gain by criticizing work that can no longer be changed by you. Even if the agency tells you they are unhappy with the copy, don't tell them you dislike it. After all, they created it and want you to think highly of them. Simply say that you hope you can help them obtain copy they are happier with in the future.

The point here is not to be dishonest and withhold your true feelings, but to be sensitive to the people who created the work and to recognize that as a "new kid on the block" you can't possibly fully appreciate the steps and frustrations that led to the final advertising product being presented to you.

Use your first meeting with the agency to obtain a feeling

for the atmosphere of the agency. While on your tour, look to see whether people are frantic or relaxed. Do they rush by in the hallways or do they look at you and maybe even smile? Do you hear laughter anywhere?

At lunch following the meeting and tour, don't talk business. Get to know your agency people personally. Ask them about their backgrounds, where they went to school, where they're from, where they worked before. Ask them what they did over the weekend with their families or friends. Be interested in them. Tell them about yourself, your family, your interests. Ask the creative people what other work they've done that you might have seen. Ask them what they're most proud of.

With a first meeting that includes commenting on advertising created by competitors, an agency tour, and lunch, you will have more than broken the ice with your agency people; you will have begun working together—collaborating.

If the agency or key agency account people are new to the business, but you are not, the same review can still take place. You may need to be brought up to date on competitive copy, and the agency people will learn the business by assembling the review. If only creative people are new to the business, it is usually the job of the account group to brief them. Some exceptions are made when the creative people must meet with R&D to understand a complicated product or when they need to see how a client's service functions.

If you follow the preceding seven steps, you will have begun to establish the collaborative environment in which your agency can create its best advertising.

CASE 10.
The Self-Fulfilling Prophecy

YOU ARE: A product manager on a new product.
THE PROBLEM: Your company has just given an assignment for a new product to an agency with which it has never worked. You have been badly burned on cost inefficiency on a different product; therefore, you would like to start this new relationship off on the right foot. Your company has arranged a fee system with your new agency

whereby you pay all the agency's time and overhead costs plus a factor for profit.

You are obviously on a very tight budget and often drive from the suburbs, where your company is located, to the agency in the city so that you won't have to pay for the agency people's driving time.

Recently, as part of their initial creative exploratory, the agency presented five storyboards when you had asked for only three. In your opinion, but not the agency's, three of the campaigns were off strategy. Nevertheless, two campaigns were tested and one was a clear winner.

Now you would like a print version of the winning television campaign. You and your product group have written a headline and visual and presented it to the agency to execute. The agency has agreed but want to do their own print ad in addition to yours. They have said they would pay for its development. You don't want them to because you and your company believe that the agency will bury its costs in the time sheets and you will end up paying anyway.

In this complex case, what did the advertiser do right and wrong? What did the agency do right and wrong? What should be done to make this relationship more productive?

chapter 7

How to get things done: A guide to day-to-day management

The creation of advertising can be exciting and fun. But the work involved in approving and producing the advertising on time and within the budget can be staggering. Even a single magazine advertisement can require at least six meetings before it is released to the magazine: one to discuss strategy and direction, three as the advertisement is presented through the layers of management (more if revisions are necessary), one to approve the mechanical, and one to approve the proof. A budget for the production of the advertisement must be developed and approved; each expenditure along the way, such as typesetting and photography, must be controlled to stay within the budget. A production schedule must also be developed and adhered to if the advertisement is to make its magazine closing dates. Finally, all of the above assumes that a media plan, including the magazines for which the advertisement is being prepared, has already proceeded through its own series of meetings and approvals.

How you manage the day-to-day work with the agency will not only determine your effectiveness in getting things done, but also will further or hinder the relationship you are building with the agency. The work you ask the agency to do and how you ask them to do it all should be within the framework of collaboration.

According to Booz • Allen & Hamilton: "The perpetually squeaky client tends to get greased, but he does not get the willing and dedicated help—nor the best breaks—nor the best creative talent—nor the collaboration he seeks. He cannot *control* inside the agency—and any efforts to do so could be evaded easily. Such a client appears likely to get less than he thinks—and probably a short life with the agency, if it is good enough not to need his business."[1]

THE AGENCY'S RESPONSIBILITIES

In *Management and Advertising Problems,* published by the Association of National Advertisers, Booz • Allen & Hamilton cited five patterns of responsibility that advertisers have delegated to their agencies. The amount of responsibility was determined by the importance of advertising to the advertiser's business and the amount of marketing work the agency performed for the advertiser. For example, in many industrial companies whose target audience is the trade rather than consumers, sales are made as a result of a salesman's call. Advertising, if it is used at all, simply creates awareness to set up the salesman's call. However, in packaged-goods marketing, sales are often made as a direct result of a consumer's exposure to advertising on television or in a magazine. Therefore, advertising is far more important to the total marketing mix.

The five patterns of agency responsibility observed by Booz • Allen & Hamilton were:

- Limited to advertising.
- Advertising plus selected services.
- Marketing counsel.
- Marketing partnership.
- Marketing leadership (agency functions as the advertiser's marketing department).[2]

Before you ask your agency to undertake any assignment, you need to understand the pattern of responsibility delegated to your agency by your company. Your source of this information is your agency contract and your management. A good rule of thumb to follow, however, in any pattern except marketing leadership, is that the agency should only be asked to do work that is related to the development of advertising and media. The creation of advertising is an agency's primary job and is the reason they were hired in the first place.

> The basic job of an agency is to create, produce, and place effective advertising. Period. In assessing whether a particular agency's service or area of involvement has worth, all you have to do is ask yourself one question: "Will it lead to better advertising?" If the answer is no, don't bother them with it. . . . Each agency has a certain amount of time to devote to its clients, and it will devote it

any way the client wants. If it's a business analysis you want, they'll analyze the pants off everything you send them. But don't ask for copy. They're too busy analyzing your business. They won't say it that way, but you'll just see a lot of bad copy. Late.

A general manager, food

It's absolutely crucial that our people know what they are supposed to do and that the agency knows what it's supposed to do. . . . I don't want my agency coming in here explaining to me that they haven't finished their media planning assignment because they've been tied up doing marketing planning support work for one of our product managers. That's the product manager's job and when he asks the agency to do it, he's making two mistakes: he's not doing his job, and he's siphoning off agency energy from the jobs they have to do and are responsible for.

An anonymous advertiser quoted by William Weilbacher in Auditing Productivity[3]

HOW TO GIVE AN ASSIGNMENT TO THE AGENCY

Think about the differences between the following two approaches to giving an assignment to an agency account executive. "John, I need an agency point of view on our recall test by the end of the week. Okay? Thanks." Versus: "John, I plan to review our recall test with my boss early next week. I'd like to present him with a joint agency-brand point of view, so do you think you could have your written comments to me by the end of this week? I hope to put a cover memo on top of your letter. What do you think?"

In the first approach, the advertiser is asking the agency to prepare an assignment in the same manner he would ask his secretary to type a report: efficiently, politely, and very appropriately for an assignment to a person who reports directly to him. Only the agency doesn't report *to* him. It works *with* him. The second approach includes many elements of a successful collaborative relationship. The advertiser gives the reason for his request, thereby making the agency feel a part of the process. By telling the agency he plans to present a joint point of view, he assures them that their opinions will be considered in the final decision. The agency feels valued and respected. Finally, by informing the agency how he plans to proceed and asking their opinion, the advertiser opens the door for the agency to suggest a better solution. For example, the recall test could include some controversial results. The agency might feel a face-to-face meeting to discuss the results would be more productive in the long run, and they could offer to be present to help the client present his case. In the second approach, the advertiser discussed the assignment with the agency rather than telling them what to do. Discussion is what collaboration is all about.

> Discussion keeps us a team.
>
> *An assistant product manager, cigarettes*

To work more productively with your agency, follow a few guidelines when giving an assignment. First, think before you call. Make sure you understand the assignment and all its ramifications before you contact the agency. Try to anticipate their questions. Know what is needed, why, and when. Second, learn precisely the work that an agency must perform to complete an assignment. If, for example, you want to know how much money a competitor spent in a test market during its first year, learn that the agency media department may be responsible for generating the information, and they may need a day or two just to begin the work. Although obtaining the information may be relatively easy, the agency may want to analyze the data and send you a letter. Therefore, if you only want one number, fast, tell your agency. Learn, too, that a small coupon advertisement for two newspapers in one market may take as much time to prepare as a magazine advertisement.

> I don't think clients appreciate how much time is spent on their business. How much time is spent thinking up the ideas, rejecting things, talking about it. Internal meetings. I don't think clients realize how much they're getting for their money . . . it seems so simple when we present an ad. There's a lot more behind it. All the decisions. All the fights.
>
> *Bob Neuman, Senior Vice President, Associate*
> *Creative Director, Backer & Spielvogel*

Set priorities with your agency. They have a limited number of people they can assign to your account, and those people have a limited amount of time. Work with your account people to decide which projects are to get immediate attention and which can wait. However, you should also be aware that work can be done very quickly in an emergency. In advertising production, money buys time. In the production of a print advertisement, for example, production time can be cut by a third. Many typesetting houses, engravers, retouchers, and illustrators will work through the night for a hefty fee. Agency people, too, will put in many hours of overtime to help you in an emergency. Their motivation is based on their being in a service business, on the relationship you have built with them, and on their desire to help you out as long as requests are reasonable and appreciated.

> If they know you're working hard and have set realistic timetables as much as you can . . . even if people have to do things overnight, if they know that you appreciate and understand, that it's not the normal thing, they may not like it, but they do it. I've found that people have come through.
>
> *A product manager, food*

> When I had been here a short amount of time and I heard somebody haranguing one day about "the agency didn't get this done overnight; the agency didn't get that done overnight" and a department in this company cannot finish projects in twelve months. I looked at that person and I said: "Why is it we so easily and handily make excuses for our own and expect the agency to meet totally unrealistic due dates and get mad when they don't? And that person said to me: "That's a very good question."
>
> *A product manager, health and beauty aids*

Once you have given the agency an assignment, try not to change directions unless it is absolutely necessary. Again, this is a management rule that applies to the advertiser-agency relationship. When the direction of an assignment is changed after work has begun, the enthusiasm of the worker and the quality of the work both suffer.

CONTINUING AGENCY ASSIGNMENTS

There are five ongoing assignments that are usually delegated to the agency no matter what the overall pattern of responsibility your company has established with the agency.

Writing and disseminating conference or "call" reports. These are written and delivered usually within 48 hours after a meeting or telephone conversation has taken place. The purpose of a conference report is to confirm in writing the action that has been agreed to by both the advertiser and agency. It is not the minutes of the meeting or conversation; it does not state what took place. It is the summation of what action will take place, by whom, and when.

Preparation of agency project lists.   Once a month, the agency should prepare a list of the status of each project in which the agency is involved. The purpose of the list is to keep both advertiser and agency up to date on the progress of each project and when work is to be expected.

Budgets.   It is usually the agency's responsibility to provide the advertiser with monthly reports on both his media and production budgets. The budgets include how much money has been spent—in which media and for production of which advertisement—and how the money still available has been allocated.

Competitive analyses.   Under many advertiser-agency contracts, it is the agency's responsibility to prepare quarterly or semiannual reports on both the media spending and advertising of the advertiser's competitors. It is also the agency's responsibility to forward new competitive information as it becomes available, be it a new commercial or a new spending level. Your agency probably subscribes to some of the many services that monitor national and local media spending and advertising by all companies.

Postanalyses.   Many advertisers ask their agencies to forward reports on the efficiency of media planning and purchasing. In broadcast, an analysis would include a comparison of planned versus delivered gross rating points and a comparison of estimated versus actual cost efficiencies. In print, an analysis might include the positions obtained for your advertising—

opposite editorial, in the front or back of the publication—plus relevant readership information if it differs from estimates on which the publication was purchased.

ALLOWING ENOUGH LEAD TIME

One of the biggest problems advertisers and agencies face in the creation, production, and placement of advertising is allowing enough lead time for the work to be completed. This is not as big a problem if the work only involves the account group or the media department. Their work is often defined, and the account and media people can usually estimate how much time a given project will take them. Also, if necessary, account and media people can put in longer hours to get the work done. However, creative people have a totally different problem because they can't be sure how long it will take to think of an idea. It can be instantaneous, occurring the moment a creative person is briefed on an assignment, or it can take months, which is unacceptable.

When the agency is working on a creative assignment, the account executive will develop a schedule that includes the date on which the work is due to you. The date is determined by the closing of the print media to be used or the air date in broadcast media. Closing dates are usually far ahead of the date on which your advertising will appear. Typical closing dates are as follows:

- Magazines (black-and-white): 2–6 weeks.
- Magazines (color): 2½–3 months.
- Television: 10 days.
- Radio: 2 days.
- Newspapers: 2 days.

To develop a schedule, the account executive works backward from the closing date or air date, allowing time for production (see schedules on page 85), time for approval by all advertiser and agency layers, time for testing, if applicable, and subtracting those weeks from the date on which the advertising schedule is being prepared. That should leave two to three weeks for the creation of the advertising or you will not make the closing or air dates, you will incur overtime, or both.

TABLE 2
Sample Development and Production Schedule

Television Commercial

	Weeks
Creation of commercials	2–3
Presentation to product manager, revisions and re-presentation	2
Presentation to group product manager, revisions and re-presentation	2
Presentations to management (three to five levels depending on the company)	2–4
Casting, preparation time	2
Preproduction	1
Shooting and editing	2
Rough-cut approvals	1–2
Final mixing, opticals, and approvals	2–3
Duplication of tapes and shipment to stations	1–2
Total	17–23

TABLE 3
Sample Development and Production Schedule

Magazine Advertisement

	Weeks
Creation of advertisement	2–3
Presentation to product manager, revisions and re-presentation	1–2
Presentation to group product manager, revisions and re-presentation	1–2
Presentation to two management levels	1–3
Photography	1–2
Retouching	1
Mechanical preparation and approval	1
Engraving (color)*	3
Total	11–17

*Black-and-white engraving: 3–5 days

Even though the pressure of time helps the creative juices to flow, and creative people can come up with outstanding advertising quickly on occasion, you will never get the best advertising from your agency if you ask for instant thinking. Even if the creative people do have an instant idea, it may not be their best; thinking about it further could improve it.

Agencies need at least two to three weeks to create advertising. Ideas often need an incubation period. A writer and art director can receive an assignment and then not think about it consciously for a while, yet they are subconsciously working on the resolution of the advertising problem. One day they'll be at the movies or walking down the street and suddenly they will have an idea. Additionally, agency creative people are usually assigned to more than one account. Accounts are not continually in need of creative work, but more importantly, a variety of advertising challenges stimulates creative thinking for all the challenges. If a creative person works on only one account, she may grow stale faster.

> The reason my copy is good is that we get out far enough in front of what we need that we're never under the gun generally. . . . We have plenty of time to develop backup copy, look at alternate strategies . . . and people have time to think.
>
> *A product manager, food*

You should also be aware, however, that even when you have allowed two or three weeks for the creation of advertising, on occasion your agency may still not have the work finished to their satisfaction. They may ask to postpone the creative presentation for a few days. Although you may feel frustrated, if the agency can still make the closing dates without you incurring overtime, try to understand why they are late. You could be trading off two days of lateness for better advertising.

MEETINGS, MEETINGS, MEETINGS

In a joint study conducted by the Association of National Advertisers and the American Association of Advertising Agencies in 1980, advertisers cited "holding too many unproductive/unnecessary meetings" as one of the major hindrances to a productive advertiser-agency relationship.[4] However, the frequency with which unnecessary meetings are held is in indirect proportion to the distance advertiser and agency must travel to meet. Midwestern advertisers with a New York City agency hold fewer, more productive meetings than advertisers in the same city as their agency. Since agencies are likely to do the majority of the traveling for meetings, simply because advertising is a service business, you need to account not only for the agency's time spent at the meeting but also their travel time to get to your office.

When arranging meetings, ask yourself whether you are making the best use of the agency's time. Could the meeting agenda be accomplished on the telephone? Often, the answer will be no. On occasion, however, the agency's time will be used more productively by not holding a meeting.

AGENCY EVALUATIONS

Many major advertisers formally evaluate their agency's performance annually or semiannually. The content of the evaluations varies a great deal by company; however, most include a grading of the agency's advertising, both as to its effectiveness and the breadth of alternatives presented; account group responsiveness to advertiser requests; calibre of marketing counsel, if appropriate; timeliness of project completion; and performance of the media, research, and accounting departments.

Agencies are extremely concerned about their evaluations because this formalized "report card" on their performance is read by the top management of their clients. It can determine whether the agency is assigned additional accounts by the advertiser.

Often the evaluations are written by middle management, but occasionally they are the responsibility of the product manager. If you must write the agency evaluation, you will once again be in the position of judging the work of your collaborators. Therefore, above all, try to be fair and professional. Praise the agency for their successes. Point out the faults in a constructive way so that they can improve their performance in the next evaluation period. Try to discuss the evaluation with your agency before forwarding it up the line to management. Collaborate on the evaluation as you do on the creation of advertising and the development of media plans. If your agency people are professionals, they understand the evaluation process

and respect your role. Criticism is accepted about their performance in the same manner it is accepted about copy. However,
should you choose to use the evaluation process unfairly to make
you look good or simply as a power trip, you will in one stroke
destroy the agency's enthusiasm, and without their personal
commitment, you will get far from their best advertising.

MAINTAINING OPEN, HONEST COMMUNICATION

It's dangerously easy to slip into the habit of not communicating
honestly with your agency. Perhaps it begins by asking the
agency for a point-of-view letter a week before you actually need
it, or not giving your true reaction to a piece of copy because you
don't want to hurt the creative people's feelings. However the
habit begins, communication is a serious problem in the advertiser-agency relationship—so serious that in January of
1982, the Main Meal Division of General Foods organized a conference with all of its agencies to collaborate on how communication between General Foods and its agencies could be
improved.

The conference was organized by Victor Elkind, manager of
development of the Main Meal Division. "The conference came
from the belief that some people were having a lot of trouble
talking straight to each other. There was a lot of encoding and
decoding of communication. At times you would sit in a meeting
and nine people would be there, and half an hour later they'd
break and the agency would leave. Then someone would turn to
someone else and say: 'Wasn't that just awful?' Now the agency
never heard that. What the agency heard was 'What I like about
the copy is this, this, this. My concerns are this, this, this.' But
there was no emotional summation of the way people felt about
the copy, which left the agency at a serious disadvantage. They
were being harshly judged with no chance to respond or even to
know that things weren't going well."

During his opening speech at the conference, Elkind elabo-
rated:

All too often, our meetings are characterized by ineffective communication. It is caused by people not saying what they feel and think. It is caused by people being frightened to take a position . . . by people worried about looking stupid . . . by people worried about getting people angry with them . . . by hidden agendas . . . by intimidation. . . . There are a lot of reasons for it. Some would argue good reasons. I would argue not good enough. In the old days . . . it was a regular occurrence for a product person and an agency person to go out drinking together after a tough meeting. After two or three martinis, they began to rehash the meeting. By this time, things are a little bit straighter, defenses are down, and understandings are reached. . . . But let me tell you what the two problems with that old technique are: One, generally, some of the people who were at the meeting didn't go along for drinks, so they missed the straight talk, or they got it—later—secondhand. Secondly, not everybody's copy judgment is enhanced by three martinis. Nonetheless, for all its deficiencies, I think it was better than what we do now! . . . I guess my wish is that we could learn to communicate in our real meetings with "three-martini straightness" and "zero-martini rationality."

Elkind believes that positive changes emerged from the conference, including more open communication among participants, the scheduling of regular meetings among agency and advertiser upper management, and a copy training program for junior advertisers.

To maintain open, honest communication with your agency day to day, follow these two simple rules, which apply to advertiser and agency alike: Say what you mean and listen.

We sometimes fail to listen. Nowhere is this more disastrous than in the personal relationships between agency and client. Historically, this breakdown has been cited time and again as the most frequent cause for account changes.

Franklin E. Schaffer, Chairman of the Board,
Doremus & Co.[5]

PROBLEMS THAT HINDER DAY-TO-DAY COLLABORATION

Inferior agency people assigned to your business.
One of the best ways to ensure that the agency assigns its

best talent to your business is to manage your agency well. Collaborate with your agency people; be open to all their ideas; support them. An agency will assign its best people to accounts where their work is implemented. An agency isn't going to waste its best brains on a client who always wants the advertising his way. However, on occasion, the agency will assign a person to your account who simply is not good enough. The agency may have hired that person in the belief that he was good, but he did not live up to expectations, or he may have capabilities better suited to another account within the agency.

Whatever the reason, you may at some time in your career be faced with the difficult situation of having to ask for the removal of an agency person from your business. This is a serious problem for both the agency person and you. The agency person could lose his job. You could gain the reputation of being hard to work with and lose the agency's respect.

Because your request for removal reflects almost as much on you as it does on the person whose removal you are requesting, you should ask for removal only as a last resort. If you are having problems with a creative person, discuss those problems with your account executive. If you're frustrated, chances are the account executive is, too. In a large agency, where creative people are reassigned to accounts on a regular basis, it may be relatively easy to assign new creative people to your business. However, if you are having problems with the account person, you should try to work out those problems on a one-on-one basis. Be as open as you can. Be specific. Keep a list. Then discuss the problems over a drink or at lunch.

If, after your discussion and a reasonable period of time, the account person's performance has not improved, bring the problem to your boss's attention. He may have a more objective view. He may even see areas where you are contributing to the difficulties. Finally, after several months, if the problem is not resolved, you should ask your boss to talk to the account person's supervisor. You yourself should not speak with your counterpart's supervisor. Removal of an account person is a sensitive situation, and it is easier for all involved if strict reporting lines are adhered to.

When a formal request for removal is made, the agency may

react in one of three ways. First, if you are an advertiser with whom the agency has been working for many years and whom they respect, they may quickly remove that person from your business. If they share your views about him, they may fire him. If they have the capability, they may transfer him to another account and give him another chance. Second, they may ask for time to work with the person to improve his weaknesses. This is the most frequent agency response. Or, third, the agency may refuse to remove the person from your business, believing that the problems are caused mainly by you. They may discuss the problem with your boss, and you may end up in more difficulty than the person whose removal you have requested.

The problem of having an inferior account person assigned to your business further emphasizes the paradox of being a client of an agency with very little authority over their work and behavior. In the above situation, you can request the removal of an account person. Sometimes your request will be complied with, sometimes not. But either way, you put yourself out on a limb because it is part of your job to work well with the agency people assigned to your account.

Frequent personnel changes. Both advertisers and agencies use reassignment as a means of training their people. However, although this practice can bring fresh thinking to marketing problems and certainly provides broad experience, it also causes lack of continuity and disrupts the advertiser-agency collaborative process. In 1975, Richard N. Courtice, then vice president of advertising and promotion at Kraft, cited lack of continuity as a reason for Kraft's problems in reviewing its agency relationships. "In the past 12 months, there have been 61 agency changes on the Kraft account and we've made 36 changes inside the Kraft organization."[6]

There is no doubt that too much turnover at both the advertiser and agency can jeopardize communication, the collaborative relationship, and ultimately the advertising created. That is why, at high levels, agencies try to maintain continuity of people. However, at lower levels, an advertiser may find herself working with new agency people every year or so. Continuity is a problem that may not go away. You may often find yourself repeating the seven steps to establishing a collaborative relationship.

Now that you understand what a collaborative relationship is, how to establish and work within it on a day-to-day basis, you're ready to review the advertising development process. Chapters 8 through 12 will teach you how to brief the agency, review the advertising presented to you, obtain approval of the advertising, and manage the print and broadcast production of your advertising.

NOTES—CHAPTER 7

1. Booz • Allen & Hamilton, Inc., "Management & Advertising Problems in the Advertiser-Agency Relationship" (New York: Association of National Advertisers, Inc., 1965), p. 115.
2. Ibid., pp. 43–58.
3. William M. Weilbacher, *Auditing Productivity* (New York: Association of National Advertisers, Inc., 1981), pp. 12–13.
4. William M. Weilbacher, *op. cit.*, pp. 102–105.
5. Franklin E. Schaffer, "The Best and Worst in Advertiser/Agency Relationships" (New York: 1975 Annual Meeting, Association of National Advertisers, Inc.), p. 16.
6. Richard N. Courtice, "The Best and Worst in Advertiser/Agency Relationships" (New York: 1975 Annual Meeting, Association of National Advertisers, Inc.), p. 9.

CASE 11.
Cancellation

YOU ARE: An account supervisor.
THE PROBLEM: The agency's presentation of a print advertisement is already almost two weeks late. You are just ready to drive to the client's company when you learn that the advertisement you had seen and approved the previous evening has been changed by the creative director. Although the basic direction of the advertisement is good, you believe that many strategic elements are missing. Should you present the advertisement or postpone the meeting?

chapter **8**

Getting the creative process off on the right foot

The creative process can be divided into six major steps:

- Briefing the agency.
- Strategy development.
- Media plan development.
- Advertising development.
- Approval—including review and testing.
- Production.

Although you play a crucial role in strategy development and the approval process, your most active, contributory role in the development of outstanding advertising is in the first step of the creative process: briefing the agency. What you get out of the agency is directly related to what you put in. If you give your agency every fact about your product or service, about the market and its consumers, and present them with a stimulating challenge, you will get back far more effective advertising than if you just hand them a copy strategy.

Briefing the agency is the beginning of a long, expensive process. Thousands of dollars will be spent to create and produce the advertising, and millions may be spent in the media to run it. Therefore, a well-planned, fact-filled briefing is worth every hour or day you and your colleagues put into it.

In this chapter, a new product or service introduction will be used as the primary example of how to brief your agency. An introduction includes all of the steps in a complete briefing. If your next briefing with your agency is on an existing product or service, you may be able to skip some of the steps covered here.

PREPARING FOR YOUR BRIEFING

Virtually every advertiser interviewed for this book included in their advice to new or junior advertisers, "Think things through before you give direction to the agency." This admonition may surprise you, but superficial thinking is a habit that's easy to fall into when advertising is only one of your responsibilities and other areas are demanding your attention. When preparing to brief your agency, you should review the following questions:

- What precisely do I want the agency to do?
  Examples: develop a new television campaign to defend against a new competitor; develop strategy and introductory advertising for a new product or service; pool out an existing print or television advertisement; develop advertising based on a new claim.
- What information do they need?
  Examples: product research, marketing research, competitive information, product samples, field trips, new research.
- What questions are they likely to ask?
  About your product or service, about competitors, about consumers, about legal restrictions.

Coordinating information for a briefing is time-consuming, but the agency is totally dependent on you for the information on which they will base the advertising.

> We have a briefing for every ad. It includes reasons to buy, reference material . . . for every new piece of glass we have a description. We give them a lot of reference material. It gets their creative juices flowing. Sometimes I think they must be sick of all the information, but in the end it pays off.
>
> *Jane Steele Kaufman, Advertising Manager, Steuben Glass*

ARRANGING THE BRIEFING

An agency briefing begins with a meeting arranged and conducted by the advertiser, very often at the product manager level. All advertiser people with information directly related to the development of advertising should attend: research and development, marketing research, product group—even a representative from manufacturing, if the process contributes any product differences or benefits.

You should request that both agency account and creative people attend the briefing, even though some agencies prefer that only the account group attend. Their reason for withholding the creative people is that advertisers can give misleading direction to the creative people. Advertisers may understand the marketing problem, but they may not have the account group's abilities to translate it into a clear assignment to the creative people. If your agency has a policy that only account people attend the briefing, you may have to live with it, or you may be able to have a preliminary discussion with your account people before the briefing to reach agreement on the assignment to the agency.

However, if possible, your agency creative people should attend the briefing. It is an important source of ideas, and if they have product questions, R&D could answer them on the spot. For example, a famous story in advertising lore concerns the invention of the claim, "Dove® creams your skin while you wash." During the briefing, a scientist told the agency that Dove contained stearic acids as one of its main ingredients. "What's that?" asked the creative director. "Stearic acids are a main ingredient in face cream." "You mean there's cream in Dove?" "Dove is one-quarter cream." Thus are great advertising claims sometimes born!

A meeting with all contributors present also enhances the collaborative relationship. It is one time when all of the collaborators can work together.

It is best if the briefing meeting takes place at your company rather than at the agency. It is your company that developed the product or service to be advertised. Just being in the atmosphere where the product was invented and seeing the people involved in their home territory helps agency people to understand your company and product and stimulates their thinking.

BRIEFING THE AGENCY

Without a doubt, attending a briefing meeting on a new product or new creative assignment is one of the most exciting steps in the creative process for advertising people. Both creative and account groups like nothing better than a fresh start—a new challenge, a new opportunity to be stimulated, to wrestle with a new problem and envision its solution in the form of great advertising. You are presenting them with a new chance to contribute and succeed both professionally and personally, so the first step in briefing the agency is simply to capitalize on their anticipation.

Set a tone of excitement for the meeting. Tell your agency that you believe your product or service has every chance of being a huge success. Credit your R&D people for inventing the product, if they did. Tell your agency that you want and need outstanding advertising to sell it. If you honestly believe that your product can become number one in five years, say that too. Hold out glories for all involved—including yourself. If agency people see how committed you are, they will believe you will support them in their work, and will try harder for you.

Explain your product or service and everything you know about it. Have samples of your product at the meeting so that agency people can use it there—touch it, smell it, eat it—and have samples for them to take home to use and experience. Ask your research and development people to explain *everything* about your product: what it's made of, how it works, how it compares to competition, what tests they used to learn about the product's performance. Diagrams or equipment needed to explain the product should also be taken to the meeting, and if seeing any part of the research and development process could contribute an idea to the agency people, a separate trip to your research and development facility should be arranged after the agency briefing.

If you're advertising a service, take them on a field trip. Have them talk with your people. Overwhelm them with information.

Give them as much data as you can . . . the more information the creatives have about your product, the better off you'll be. If you're in manufacturing, take the creative people to your plant. If you have a service, let the creative people hang around your offices for a couple of days. You'll never know what little pearls a creative can see that you can't.

Mary Seggerman, Senior Product Manager, General Foods

Explain the market in which you are competing. Who's the market leader? Who are the runners-up? What are they saying in their advertising? What are the competitors' strengths and weaknesses? Bring samples of competing products for the agency to try. Where are the opportunities in the marketplace as you see them? Are there any unfulfilled needs? Are there any ways your product or service might fill these needs?

Explain your knowledge of consumer behavior in your market. Using all the marketing research available to you— attitude and usage studies, segmentation studies—explain, or ask your marketing research people to explain, why consumers purchase the brands and types of products or services within your category, how they use the products or services, what they like and dislike. Explain which consumers you see as your most likely target. Then give the research studies to the agency people to review. Their interpretation may differ from yours and give new direction to the solution of your marketing problem, or a detail in the research could stimulate a big advertising idea.

Define the problem, not the solution. Give your agency clear direction on what you want them to do, but don't tell them how to do it. This is extremely important. For example, if you are introducing a new toy, do not show your agency a competitor's advertisement that uses an emotional theme and ask them to copy it. The agency may analyze the problem and conclude that an educational approach may be best for selling your toy. You may be right or they may be right, but if you present a solution as you are presenting the problem, you are hurting your advertising two ways: First, you may be steering the agency away from what could be a better solution than yours. Second, you are asking the agency to either agree or disagree with you before they've even begun the creative process. At this stage, neither you nor the agency knows the answer.

Learning how to give the problem and not the solution may be difficult at first. In your day-to-day work with your management, you are striving to do just the opposite—present the solutions, not problems—but you should keep trying.

> Sometimes it's hard not to visualize the solution when you give an assignment to the agency.
>
> *Abby Kohnstamm, Director of Industry Marketing,*
> *American Express*

> A lot of clients, as soon as they start to formulate the problem, know how they want to solve it. And that gets to be a problem for us. Especially when you present a solution and they say "Well, that's not the way I saw it."
>
> *A copywriter*

Explain restrictions, if any.   In the area of toys, drugs, and sanitary protection, in particular, there are strong government and industry regulations on advertising. (See Chapter 10.) You or your lawyer should cover these regulations with the agency at the briefing. If there are specific claims for your product or service that can or cannot be made, explain them in detail, and try to give your reasons why. If your company has any policies about advertising, explain them, too. For example, some companies will not run advertising in which their product or service is compared directly to a named or unnamed competitor. Finally, if you have any budgetary restrictions on the advertising, cover them at the briefing meeting. You don't want your agency to create a print advertisement that costs $20,000 to produce when your budget is only $10,000.

Expect the unexpected from agency questions.   Encourage the agency to ask questions at the briefing and then be prepared to see immediately the new kind of thinking they bring to the marketing process. Their questions will be your first challenge to yourself to keep an open mind, to present the problem and not the solution, to encourage the broadest possible thinking even though an agency question makes you afraid that they may be headed in the wrong direction.

Try to make the briefing a dialogue instead of a lecture. At the beginning of the collaborative process, there should be as few *no's* as possible, and even though your tendency may be to control, try to remember that although you have lived with the marketing problem for a few months, it's new to the agency. It is precisely their fresh thinking, their consumer viewpoint, that could bring you an innovative, effective advertising solution to the problem.

Stretch your creative people.   If you want advertising that is truly outstanding, sells your product, and with which you are proud to be associated, encourage your agency to come up with totally new ideas, to aim for advertising solutions that have never been tried before.

> A good client encourages you to try new things all the time. . . . They're always encouraging you to stretch. . . . they're very receptive to things that are not necessarily extensions of what they've done in the past.
>
> *Bernard Rosner, Vice President, Creative Director, Ogilvy & Mather Partners*

> What the creative people want out of the business is personal reward. . . . They want to solve the problem and take on the creative challenge you've handed them. I think it's important to . . . extend the challenges to them to the point that they're being stretched, being challenged, because I think they get a lot of personal satisfaction out of that.
>
> *Ronald Leong, Group Product Manager, Bristol-Myers*

Give your agency lots of leeway.   Once you've given your agency information and clear direction on what you want them to do, back off and let them come up with all the ideas they can, no matter how unrealistic these ideas may seem at the beginning. You can always edit an idea later, but an idea dismissed prematurely may be gone forever.

Give them guidance, then provide them with the broadest and most comfortable creative environment.

Richard Rosenbloom, Vice President,
Advertising, Card Division, American Express

I think the same thing works best with an agency as with anyone you work with—you need to be very clear about your expectations, your values, and your criteria so that people have a fair chance to try and do good work for you. My experience is, given the economics of the business, most people are terrifically motivated and pretty capable. . . . If you've really been clear about what you want from people and give them a fair chance to contribute, it creates an environment that maximizes the chance of success for everyone involved.

Victor Elkind, Development Manager, Main
Meal Division, General Foods

Finally, don't change direction. You should have thought through your direction to the agency so carefully that there is no chance you will have to change it once the agency is briefed. It is difficult for any creative person to maintain the enthusiasm necessary to create great advertising if direction is changed.

I think the worst clients are those who change direction all the time because they don't know what they're doing. Anytime they talk to someone they realize they'd better change direction to the agency or the agency will do a lousy job and they'll look stupid.

Tracy Kelly, Product Manager, Bristol-Myers

The creative process is like archery. The client should set up the target somewhere and place it firmly. Don't move it. I can't hit a moving target.

Jeff Atlas, Copywriter, Ogilvy & Mather

You lose steam. You just lose spirit. After a while, you just know that it's going to be an exercise . . . that they really and truly don't know what they want. That you have to go through this phenomenal process of elimination before they ever decide what they want rather than them deciding up front; you just get so demoralized and the work slacks off. It's just not as good. I remember one client (who will remain nameless) coming out of a big presentation. Eight campaigns and eight selling lines. Eight big campaigns. "Love the work. We'll get back to you." Within a week, it was all dead. Gear up again for another presentation in three weeks. . . . It's just awful. And I don't mind doing a lot of work . . . you've just got to have people you know are going to be responsive and know what they want and can recognize good work.

A copywriter

STRATEGY DEVELOPMENT

If your briefing to the agency has been for a new product or service, a new claim for an existing product or service, or you are involved in a restage, your next step is the development of a positioning and creative strategy. You should already know from your reading of the fundamentals of advertising that determining a positioning and creative strategy for your product or service are two crucial marketing decisions. As a reminder, these terms are defined below.

Positioning.   The place your product or service holds in the consumer's mind. It is the one fact by which the product or service is known. Complete the following sentence and you will know the positioning for Ivory: "Ivory® is the soap that is. . . ."

Creative strategy.   A plan for what the advertising will say and how it will say it. Creative strategies can differ in their formats, but they all contain the following elements:

- Objective: what the advertising should do.
- Consumer benefit(s).
- Support for the benefit(s).
- Target-audience definition.
- Advertising tone.

Because of the importance of the positioning and strategic decisions, marketing research is often used to aid those decisions—attitude and usage studies, consumer segmentation studies, even tests on competitors' advertising campaigns. Within the research, you and the agency should find information to help you ascertain the primary benefit(s) of your product or service and the most believable and unique support for the benefit(s). Research can also guide you to the age, income, education level, and psychographic attitudes of consumers who will be most likely to buy your product or service. However, the challenge presented by research is in interpreting it, and in reaching agreement on the interpretation. When using research to determine positioning and strategy, you may find that not only do you and your agency disagree, but also that your management, who should approve your copy strategy prior to the agency executing it, has their own interpretation. Therefore, research conducted prior to the development of advertising often leads to several strategic directions. In that case, one or more of the following additional research techniques may be used to determine the strongest position and strategy.

Focus groups.   Discussions with consumers led by a moderator. Sample positionings may be exposed to consumers to obtain a general response. Focus groups are qualitative, not quantitative, research.

Claim or promise tests.   Quantitative research that measures the strength of simple, short declarations of product or service benefits.

Concept tests.   Quantitative research that measures the relative strength of more elaborate statements of the positioning and strategy. Concepts can be tested in the form of concise paragraphs or concept advertisements with visuals.

The development and approval of a positioning and strategy can take many months, but it is a particularly exciting time for everyone involved in the collaborative relationship, for the reason that there are no right answers yet. Advertiser, account, and creative people may attend focus groups together and then discuss what they've learned. All are searching, making intuitive guesses, contributing ideas—*collaborating*—and because many statements can be tested in a claim or concept test, everyone has a chance to learn the strength of his own ideas.

Strategy development is what keeps me in the advertising business. It is my favorite part of the whole process. I just love gathering all the facts, then getting a group of sharp people together and hassling and arguing and joking until we've come up with some alternate strategies.

A vice president, account supervisor

MEDIA PLAN DEVELOPMENT

Once the advertiser and agency have agreed on a creative strategy, the agency will involve the media department to develop a media strategy. You should be aware from your reading of media fundamentals that a media strategy includes determining which media will best meet marketing objectives, which will reach the target market most efficiently, and which can execute the creative strategy most effectively. Obviously, the creative group cannot begin advertising development until they know whether broadcast or print media will be used and the length of the commercial message or size of the print advertisement.

The creative use of media includes not only reaching the target audience the optimum number of times during purchase periods, and in the appropriate editorial or program environment, but also utilizing the strengths of each medium to communicate product or service benefits. The benefits of some can be most effectively communicated on television—a product that can be demonstrated, such as a food processor, or a service that can be dramatized, such as overnight delivery service. For other products or services, print can be most effective. Automobiles use print to communicate a full product story that cannot be told in 30 or 60 seconds. Some food products use magazines to provide recipes that expand the uses of the products. Sanitary-protection products use print because broadcast standards allow only general descriptions of the product benefits.

The details of the development of an effective media strategy are beyond the scope of this book; however, when proceeding through the creative-development process you need to be aware that the choice of media affects the advertising and the creative strategy affects the choice of media.

THE WAITING PERIOD

After you have briefed the agency, have worked your way through positioning and strategy development, it is time for the agency creative people to be left alone to create the advertising. The waiting period could be as short as two weeks or as long as four or five. Although it might be tempting to pick up the phone and ask the creative people how they're doing, resist! The creative people need time by themselves to solve the problem their way. The account people need time to review the advertising and maybe suggest some additional directions to the creative people. You should be available to answer questions, and maybe once or twice ask your account people how things are progressing, but your main function at this point in the creative process is simply trusting—and preparing yourself for the big meeting when the agency presents the creative work to you.

CASE 12.
"It Comes When It Comes"

YOU ARE: President of a small company.
THE PROBLEM: You need to put together a timetable to introduce a new service. You have called the agency account executive for a schedule on advertising development. She has said: "We at ABC advertising understand your time concerns, but we do not believe in committing to rigid timetables. Creative comes when it comes."
    What should you do?

---

chapter **9**

How to review advertising—even if you don't know a good idea when you see one

Recognizing great advertising is equal in importance to creating great advertising. That's part of your job, and it isn't easy. You can learn all the rules about the ingredients of effective advertising (your company may even have a checklist for you to follow), but recognizing the undefinable spark in a commercial or print advertisement that makes it come alive, makes it instantly felt, is a skill that cannot be learned overnight. It must be developed through exposure and experience.

The one comforting thought about the difficult task of judging advertising is that nobody has perfected a way to do it. Research can aid judgment. In 1981 an estimated $53 million was spent on copy testing, according to the *New York Times*.[1] However, research doesn't always provide the answer either. The famous "Do You Know Me?"® campaign for the American Express® Card was not immediately recognized as outstanding by either advertiser or agency. It was one of three campaigns tested, and all three had statistically similar results. American Express decided to adopt "Do You Know Me?" basically on judgment.

Advertising is part art, part science—and probably more art than science because of the emotional buttons that must be pushed to persuade a consumer to purchase a product or service. Therefore, judging advertising, like judging art, is highly intuitive and subjective. More important than knowing the rules is learning how to understand and trust your own reactions to advertising. Prior to testing, there are no numbers to help you recognize good advertising. *Judging advertising isn't like making any other business decision.*

Kids coming out of business school . . . think an advertising problem is susceptible to the same kind of analytical techniques that a financial problem is susceptible to, and it isn't. That's why you get a lot of clients asking an agency for fifteen options. Because they're taught in school that decisions are made by sifting through options. But what they don't appreciate is that you can't get a good creative person to write fifteen storyboards when all he likes is one. You can tell him what you like and what you don't like about the one he's made. But if you send him away to bring back fifteen so you can pick from fifteen, he will go and work on somebody else's business.

A general manager, food

In judging copy, follow instincts, follow your gut feeling about the copy rather than trying to judge copy by a list of items. Business school doesn't teach you how to judge copy, and there's no way to teach anyone how to judge copy. You can learn that there should be certain things in copy, but there's no way to really learn how to judge it except by instincts.

Susan Hudson, Vice President, Account
Supervisor, Ogilvy & Mather

They should throw away all the stuff they learn in the courses to be an MBA and they should be open-minded. . . . There's no school for judging advertising. You just have to have something within you that says, "That's it! I know my product. I know how they make it. I know who it will appeal to—that's it!" It's trusting your feelings.

Bob Neuman, Senior Vice President, Associate
Creative Director, Backer & Spielvogel

Problems in this world are never solved in strictly logical terms. While logic may be part of the solution, it's never the whole thing. Remember advertising in the seventies? It had become utterly and totally dependent upon logic. No wonder so much of it was awful. Many things in life are dependent upon emotion, too. The consumer is a human being who may be able to accept a logical reason why she should buy this or that product. But she's also emotional. She needs to be romanced . . . loved . . . cared for . . . entertained . . . charmed. She really *needs* it. Yet, many times I've sat in meetings where someone has said "TELL ME WHY! Give me a logical reason!" You can't always do that.

Malcolm End, Senior Vice President, Creative
Director, Ogilvy & Mather

Everything you've just read is telling you to think, feel, and work in a way that is very different from the other thought processes of a product manager or owner of a small business. You have been told to use your *personal* judgment instead of following usual business procedures. As you learn to trust your personal reactions, you will become more comfortable judging advertising; however, your first creative review may be an intimidating experience. You know your comments are being judged by your colleagues and superiors as well as by the agency. You know that in your first few exposures to advertising, there is little chance you can make major contributions, and a good chance that you can make a fool of yourself. Some people interviewed for this book went so far as to recommend that junior clients not speak at copy reviews:

> My advice to assistant brand managers is that they should learn to keep their mouths shut.
>
> *A copywriter*

> The best suggestion I can give to people just starting out in any business, whether it's advertising or the client side, is to be very careful how they comment. There are too many cases where an assistant product manager opens his or her mouth and gets his or her foot placed down in it.
>
> *A group product manager, health and beauty aids*

Of course, you can never go wrong choosing your comments carefully in a copy review no matter what your level, but if you remain silent at a copy review, you will never learn to trust your own judgment. You should certainly do a lot of listening, but also some speaking.

> What I tell these people is "Trust your judgment. If it's bad, get into a line of work where your judgment is better. If it's good, you'll get rich and famous fast."
>
> *A general manager, food*

> People at the assistant product manager level are frequently preoccupied with not doing anything wrong. And in an effort not to do anything wrong, you don't really respond spontaneously to anything. . . . Don't just try to cover your tracks. . . . There's the other element of trying to support the things you think are right.
>
> *Bernard Rosner, Vice President, Creative*
> *Director, Ogilvy & Mather Partners*

I think some people have some image of how they should be perceived professionally and don't want to make any mistakes or ask dumb questions. I think you've got to throw all that out the window or you're never going to learn. . . . If you make a dumb comment, my feeling is you'll be forgiven for it. And if someone sets your mind straight, you'll never forget it.

John Deford, Product Manager, Colgate

PREPARING FOR THE CREATIVE REVIEW

Nowhere is maintaining the collaborative relationship with your agency more important than in the creative review. Until this point in the advertising-creation process, you have made the majority of the contributions in briefing the agency and in helping to write and approve the strategy. Now the agency creative people have just spent two or more weeks creating the advertising for your product or service and reviewing it within the agency. The presentation to you is their moment of truth. The creative review is a dramatic meeting filled with tension, expectation, and emotion. To function best in the meeting, you need to prepare for it. Of course, you should review the strategy and your competitors' advertising. Know what you're looking for in the copy, but even more important, you should prepare your attitude.

You are in a position of power at a creative review. You are a collaborator, but you are also judging the work the agency has created. Your company expects you to comment on the copy and ask for revisions as you see fit. Even though you do not have the authority to say yes, to approve the copy for production, you can say no. However, if you want to maintain your collaboration with the agency, how you give your comments to the agency is as important as what you say. Depending on your attitude, the agency will go back to the drawing board inspired to meet the challenges you have set forth—or feeling resentful, frustrated, and defensive. Therefore, before you go into a creative review, run through this checklist of attitudes and emotions.

Try to be an advisor rather than an authority.   Help the agency to see your thoughts from your point of view, not from your position of power. Even though you often can insist that the agency do things your way, your way may not always lead to the best advertising. Remember, you are a collaborator. It is collaboration that leads to the best advertising.

> Let us do our job. They do their job. Let us do our job. . . . We can't do it without them, but they've got to give us our due and take our word.
>
> *A copywriter*

> I think they [advertisers] should, first of all, respect the position they're in. They're calling the shots. That puts a certain responsibility on their shoulders. They're ruling on somebody else's efforts and . . . they have to be very aware . . . and very sensitive. If they don't like something, they have to arm themselves with reasons the creative person can understand. Even if it boils down to a question of personal taste, they have to deal with that so the creative person comes away with some kind of guidance and is satisfied. They have to use that upper hand with delicacy.
>
> *Bernard Rosner, Vice President, Creative*
> *Director, Ogilvy & Mather Partners*

Try to be open-minded. Expect the unexpected. If you enter a creative review with specific expectations, you will be disappointed. There is no way the agency can create the advertising exactly as you imagined it, and, if you are disappointed, you may not be receptive to potentially better ideas.

> He should open his mind. The most glorious solutions are not the ones he has envisioned.
>
> *Franchellie Cadwell, President, Cadwell Davis Partners*

> Don't be afraid of new, far out, funny, whatever. Just don't be scared of new ideas. . . . Some of them [advertisers] just get their backs up if they see something out of the mold. But you know, I think there's a danger in accepting things just because they're acceptable. . . . Don't be scared of new ideas.
>
> *A copywriter*

Be prepared to give your own opinions, not your boss's. Don't second-guess. If you personally believe the advertising is good, be prepared to fight for it. If you believe changes need to be made, state them and be prepared to be right or wrong. At least then you will have contributed. If all you do is second-guess, you will have none of the satisfaction of contributing and could very well eliminate a big idea or make the advertising less effective.

Second-guessing your boss is also extremely frustrating to the agency people you are working with. If they are collaborating with you and you disagree with their advertising, they can defend their copy right then and there, but they can't change your boss's mind if she isn't present.

Finally, second-guessing is just that—*guessing*. You may incorrectly guess your boss's judgment and eliminate an advertisement she thinks is outstanding.

> The worst clients tend to be people who are more concerned about what their boss is thinking than about how the advertising really works or how the consumer's going to view the advertising. Second-guessing is probably the biggest problem.
>
> *A vice president, account supervisor*

> An inept client is usually fearful. Fear is a destroyer of good judgment. Fear is a destroyer of intuitive thinking. Fear is the problem they all deal with. Second-guessing their bosses. Never making decisions based on their own instinctive judgment or rational judgment.
>
> *Malcolm End, Senior Vice President, Creative Director, Ogilvy & Mather*

Finally, admit your discomfort to yourself.   It's hard to admit feelings of which you're not proud, but if you've been reviewing advertising for less than three years, it is highly unlikely that you're bursting with confidence. So admit your discomfort, then act on that admission by asking questions. Questioning will help you understand the advertising process better and will also make the agency rethink all the reasons why the advertising was created. Your questions may just make the advertising better.

> I was nervous [at my first creative review]. . . . I tried to be as objective as possible. I used my common sense. I didn't know what else to do. And it wasn't a question of whether I liked something

or didn't like something . . . it was "Is this communicating what we want it to communicate and what is it going to look like versus what the other guys are doing?" I think I still use that as my benchmark.

Ellen Elias, Group Product Manager, Lever Brothers

I think I felt more expert the first one or two times . . . than as the year and a half went on. Because I came from research and I was an expert there, and I just carried that mentality to this job. I was out of my domain moving into this job, but mentally I was still stuck as "an expert" with strong opinions. So I had strong opinions about the advertising. And I think it wore away after the initial two months on the job. . . . [Why?] Feeling very strongly about something that nobody else felt strongly about. I began to question my own sense of advertising judgment. Maybe I didn't know it all. Also, I was just very aware of how the copywriter and creative director were responding to my comments or not responding! It just made me stop and listen for a while and not be so opinionated. I was just not getting good vibrations from them. . . . They'd listen and then they'd move on. I wasn't comfortable until I just stopped opening my mouth so much and started to listen more and save some of my comments for behind-the-scenes conversation. . . . I found it all very difficult. Very upsetting. I think that was one of the hardest things I had to learn.

An assistant product manager, cigarettes

Admitting your discomfort and lack of expertise also helps you avoid defenses and cover-ups that are counterproductive to your primary objective: getting the best advertising from your agency. According to Booz • Allen & Hamilton: "The attempt to achieve the additional capability of creative advertising judgment—on top of general business capabilities of product managers—often proves unrealistic, resulting in uncertain and defensive attitudes in dealing with agency people, irrelevant nit-picking and compromise of creative recommendations."[2]

WHAT TAKES PLACE AT A CREATIVE REVIEW MEETING

The creative review is an exciting, high-energy, high-tension meeting. For the creative people, it's their opportunity to show you all the work they've created in the past few weeks. They're proud of it. They're excited to share their ideas with you, and especially for you to become as excited about the work as they are. It's exciting for you, too, to see the advertising that you contributed to, advertising that could make your sales leap forward. A creative review is business and show business rolled into one. In a sense, every participant is on stage: the creative people when they present the copy, the account people when they explain the recommendations to you, and you, when you give your comments.

Most creative reviews have a similar format, which can be divided into four parts:

1. The agency introduction or setup.
2. Presentation of creative work.
3. Advertiser comments.
4. Agency recommendation and discussion.

1. The Agency Setup (Usually Delivered by the Account Group)

Of course you're being set up! The agency believes that it has solved an advertising problem, and it wants you to see the solutions their way—to be as excited about the advertising as they are. If you agree with how they define the creative problems in the setup, you are more likely to agree with the solutions they present. For example, if the product is a chicken coating mix and the agency's recommended advertisement contains a demonstration, the agency setup will likely include the importance of visualizing the difference between your product and the competition.

Agency setups also often include relevant research, competitive advertising, and previous advertising for your own product or service. The purpose is to put the advertising you are about to see in the context of both the advertising problem and the larger marketing problem in order to give a rationale for each advertisement presented. The agency setup must also include a review of the creative strategy. It is the agreed-upon standard to which the advertising was written and by which it should be judged.

You should listen carefully to agency setups, but also take them with a few grains of salt. Most likely, the setup is created as carefully as the advertising itself. In fact, it is an ad for the ads.

2. Presentation of Creative Work

This part of the creative review is usually conducted by the agency copywriter and art director, who worked as a team. The creative people will introduce each commercial or print advertisement before they present. Their purpose is to have you understand how they analyzed the advertising problem to arrive at each solution. Of course, they want to convince you that the advertising is terrific, but they also want to draw you into the advertising, to involve you.

When the creative team presents each commercial or print ad, they will present the visual first and then the copy from a television storyboard or a print layout. Each piece of advertising will probably be reviewed twice before moving on. If twice isn't enough for you to understand the advertising, you can request an additional review before you give your comments.

Agencies often present more than one solution to an advertising problem, and many agencies will save their recommended solution for last. As you work with your agency, you may learn their pattern and be able to predict where they have come out!

3. Advertiser Comments

How and when comments are given depends on the advertiser and agency people at the meeting. Many advertisers and agencies prefer to review all advertising before making comments. Others prefer to comment after each advertisement or commercial is presented.

You may be the only advertiser representative at the meeting and the only person commenting, or you may be one of a group. As a general rule, junior people in an advertiser group present their comments first. This puts a burden on you, if you're a junior person. You have little time to collect your thoughts, and you have not heard other comments to guide you. However, it also gives you an opportunity to show some independent thinking and impress your superiors.

4. Recommendation and Discussion

After the agency has listened to your comments, it will present its recommendation about which advertisement or commercial should be produced and why. (A few agencies may prefer to make their recommendations immediately after the presentation of copy.) The agency will then address your and other advertiser comments and concerns. They will either agree or disagree and state their reasons why. Eventually, advertiser and agency will reach agreement on changes, the need for additional work, or proceeding to the next level of management for approval to final production.

At the end of the meeting, the most junior agency person, who will be writing the call report, should review all agreements reached. If he does not, you should ask for a recapitulation of agreements and next steps.

HOW TO REVIEW ADVERTISING

> When Judy gave us her comments, we cringed. "Change this. Add that." She never even listened to the commercial. She had her pencil out and made changes as we were presenting. But Bob, he was right with us. And when he had a change, it was up for discussion. Oh, we made Judy's changes all right, and let her live with them. They were usually bad. But with Bob, we always tried to see his problem and solve it. It wasn't their brains that made the difference, it was their attitude and way of working with us. Bob got the best out of us. Judy got nothing except her own ideas and ultimately mediocre ads.
>
> *An account supervisor*

How you give your comments to the agency is as important as the substance of the comments. Of course, the copy must be on strategy, and it must adhere to the fundamentals of good advertising, but to continually get the best advertising from your agency, you need to learn how to give your creative comments in the spirit of collaboration. Here are 14 steps to follow in the advertising review that will make your comments most effective:

REACT TO THE ADVERTISING AS A PERSON

Don't take notes the first time you see an advertisement or a commercial. Instead, pretend you're seeing the advertisement at home in a magazine or on television. Then react to it. If it's funny, laugh. Feel it and trust those initial feelings. The consumer to whom you are selling is also a person. If you let yourself react, you can trust your reactions to be indicative of your consumer's reactions. One advertiser described a commercial presented to him in which a little boy was embarrassed because he had a loose tooth. Think about that. When you had a loose tooth as a child, were you embarrassed? Probably not. You were proud because losing a tooth is a sign of growing up. The commercial was changed to show a child wearing braces, a more realistic reason for embarrassment.

> Bring your own experience to these things. If it doesn't sync with your own experience, it's probably wrong. . . . If you're bored, chances are it's boring. If it makes you smile, chances are it will make everybody smile.
>
> *A general manager, food*

> When I look at copy, I want to be personally excited by the communication. I recognize the feeling in myself because I've seen a lot of television that does it for me. . . . I've found out that I have generalizable tastes, which is a blessing in this business. When something is turning me on, it's a fair assumption that it's turning other people on, too.
>
> *Victor Elkind, Manager of Development,*
> *Main Meal Division, General Foods*

> My biggest client is a good client because he knows . . . he can look at a television commercial and know whether he likes it or not. Gut feeling or whatever, his instincts are good, and you come

away knowing that he's liked it or he hasn't liked it. And that's good. A good client is somebody who has an opinion, a point of view. Who's not just a rubber stamp.

Bernard Rosner, Vice President, Creative
Director, Ogilvy & Mather Partners

Practice being as open-minded as you can and receptive to unusual solutions. Learn to judge advertising as much with your instincts as with your intellect.

Malcolm End, Senior Vice President, Creative
Director, Ogilvy & Mather

When you react to advertising as a person, it demonstrates your involvement to the agency people. It shows that you have paid attention and have understood what they are trying to communicate. Your reaction is important to them.

At least if a client will respond . . . oh, they listen and they nod. I want to hear something! If you have reasons, tell me what they are. I'm a reasonable man, and if I'm off base, I want to know why—but this guy, he sits and sits and does not respond. And that's worse than anything.

Bob Neuman, Senior Vice President, Associate
Creative Director, Backer & Spielvogel

Whether you like their work or not, at least if you pay attention to what they're saying and don't dismiss it out of hand or say "Thanks for your input, but we're doing it my way," then I think people feel good that at least the long hours and thought that have gone into it and all the internal meetings are not for nought.

A product manager, food

Finally, reacting to the advertising as a person will help you see your product or service from the consumer's perspective. If your product is toothpaste, you spend all your workdays and many nights and weekends thinking about toothpaste. That product is your baby. However, a consumer only uses toothpaste twice a day and probably only thinks about it consciously when she's making her purchase decision. To be most effective, your advertising has to take the consumer's perspective into account.

MAKE GENERAL COMMENTS FIRST, SPECIFIC COMMENTS SECOND

If your agency has just presented six television storyboards, an appropriate first comment is not "I think the lady in the third commercial should be wearing a blue dress, not a red one." Instead, tell the agency that they have accomplished an extraordinary amount of work. Then comment on the overall range of the alternatives. Have many points of view been covered? Do the commercials represent a variety of executional techniques? Finally, focus on each commercial, and again, be general before being specific. Comment on the big selling idea behind each commercial before referring to specific words.

BE SENSITIVE TO YOUR CREATIVE PEOPLE

In Chapter 3, we discussed how copywriters and art directors must put their entire personalities into the advertising to make it come alive. No matter how professional they are, the advertising is still an extension of themselves, and when you comment on their copy, you are commenting on them personally. Most have developed professional "callouses"; however, they still feel good when you like their copy and not so good when you don't.

> It's very hard to separate the impersonal from the personal. It's easy to say "Well, I know you're not rejecting my idea" . . . but it rubs off on you. There's no way you can walk away and not feel you've been stomped on. And, in fact, the creative part of the business is the part that's the most exposed on the conference room table. Like you really lie there naked and ask that your work, which is an extension of yourself, be accepted.
>
> *Bernard Rosner, Vice President, Creative*
> *Director, Ogilvy & Mather Partners*

> Rejection is always frustrating, but you can accept that when it's reasonable.
>
> *Bob Neuman, Senior Vice President, Associate*
> *Creative Director, Backer & Spielvogel*

Understand that you're dealing with a personality who feels strongly. Respect that strength. Then, if you have problems, couch those problems in a discussion environment. If the copy isn't right, it could be your fault in guidance.

Richard Rosenbloom, Vice President, Advertising,
Card Division, American Express

BE HONEST

Creative people learn early in their careers how to accept honest criticism given with the purpose of improving the advertising. Should they feel rejected in the process, they will recover. Professionals always do. Honesty is part of your job as a collaborator. The agency needs your expertise, your point of view, to create outstanding advertising.

Capable, secure writers and art directors welcome candor. They need it. They worry about clients who are less than candid. It's the code I live by in this business. Good teammates, because of their different job functions, have different perspectives on any given subject. To create good advertising, they must listen to one another carefully and speak to one another as candidly as possible. That's what I try to do. When I'm in a meeting, I hope no one will feel it necessary to critique the advertising just for the sake of doing so. But if deep in their gut they feel something is wrong, I hope they will say so and give me their reasons why. Then I can listen carefully and digest their opinion so I can either agree or disagree. Candor is absolutely part of this process.

Malcolm End, Senior Vice President, Creative
Director, Ogilvy & Mather

My sense is that creative people like candor! If you're up front with them and say to their faces, "You know, I don't like that piece of copy," they can identify with that. *"He doesn't like it. Why?"* "I don't like the premise. It's hokey." *"He thinks the premise is hokey."* . . . Most clients don't appreciate the value of candor. They have this notion that the creative people are bringing forth a baby. They have slaved over it. It is perfect. If I criticize it, they will hate me. And if they hate me, they may hurt me. And rather than take the risk that they may hurt me, I'll just throw some meaningless words at them. . . . It comes out of fear. . . . The result is that the copy itself suffers because the honesty of communication necessary to approve it isn't there.

Victor Elkind, Manager of Development,
Main Meal Division, General Foods

Don't just be honest. Be honest in front of the agency. Don't tell them at a copy meeting that everything is wonderful, then write or phone two days later asking them to change everything. As a collaborator, you should present your point of view in a situation where that point of view can be discussed. Otherwise it becomes a dictate, and while you may have succeeded in getting your way, both the advertising and your relationship with the agency could suffer.

TAKE YOUR TIME

If you have only a general opinion about the advertising presented at the review, and you want more time to review the advertising in detail, take it. Many agencies will resist letting you study the advertising. They want an immediate reaction. However, it is illogical and unfair to expect you to react in a few minutes to work it took the agency weeks to create. Take the advertising home with you. Read it by yourself. Collect your thoughts and respond to the agency within two days, not more, so that you do not lose momentum and enthusiasm.

A creative presentation is a tough thing to handle as a product manager because you get a barrage of campaigns . . . and you may see as many as six or seven storyboards in a two-hour time frame. They give you literally two minutes to digest all of this, to pull together your thoughts, to come to a point of view. . . . It's an incredible amount to have to absorb and react to that fast. . . . I now give my initial response at the creative meeting, then I take the boards home for two days and come back with a point of view. The creative people don't like it. They are disappointed they don't get an immediate reaction.

Mary Seggerman, Senior Product Manager, General Foods

If you do take a day or two to respond to your agency, try to give your comments in person. Call another meeting. Again, in a collaborative relationship, the agency should have a chance to respond to your comments, to accept or reject them, give their reasons why, and ultimately have all collaborators reach a joint point of view.

GIVE REASONS FOR YOUR COMMENTS

Every word in a print advertisement or commercial has a reason for being there, right or wrong. Therefore, any criticism you make about the advertising must also have a reason behind it. If you do not know those reasons when you comment, or you do not state them, the agency will not be able to respond and either accept your suggestions to improve the advertising or explain why they disagree with you.

Equally as important, the agency will feel that you are arbitrarily dismissing their work. That feeling dampens enthusiasm and collaborative efforts. For example, if you are advertising a detergent and the agency has chosen a diaper as an example of how white the detergent makes fabrics, don't just say, "I don't want to use a diaper." Explain why: "Paper diapers have become so popular, I wonder whether many women can identify with a cloth diaper anymore."

> Creative people are the most valuable asset the agency has to offer. . . . When it is decided to refuse judgments, authority requires no explanation, but respect for experience and capabilities does. Creative people live to see their ideas used. They try again with enthusiasm only when the rejection is known as thoughtful, not arbitrary. In the words of one advertiser: "Give the reasons for your decisions or you will cut the heart out of the agency people."
>
> *Booz • Allen & Hamilton, Inc.*[3]

The agency respects your views if they understand your reasoning.

> *Abby Kohnstamm, Director of Industry Marketing,*
> *American Express*

A bad client is someone who can't communicate why he doesn't like an ad. You don't go to a doctor and not be able to say where a pain is. You can't cure something that you can't identify.

Jeff Atlas, Copywriter, Ogilvy & Mather

To get the best advertising from your agency, don't live by the rules. You can't make advertising by using a formula or by numbers. Follow your instincts. It's not the same as looking at a marketing proposal or sales results . . . but try to understand why you feel or react to a piece of copy. If you don't explain why, you won't be helpful to the agency.

Susan Hudson, Vice President, Account
Supervisor, Ogilvy & Mather

DON'T NITPICK

When you're new to reviewing advertising, it's easier to comment on details than to give truly constructive criticism. It's easier to say, "Shouldn't the woman be wearing a blue dress?" than to say, "Is there any way to link the benefit more closely to the reason why in frame six?" Although nit-picking is comfortable and makes you feel as if you are contributing, most often it has little or no effect on the effectiveness of the advertising. Most clients learn by experience that nit-picking does not pay off.

I used to do a lot of copy editing, a lot of which did not improve the advertising substantially at all. It only served to delay the process and possibly served to hurt the relationship. Now I take a much broader picture.

Abby Kohnstamm, Director of Industry Marketing,
American Express

My own creative philosophy is—if you develop a concept that is solid, confirm that that concept is solid, then write a strategy from that concept and execute against *that* strategy and there has been no flaw in the executional elements, diddling around with this or that word of copy can sometimes hurt the board. The agency creative people, if they're doing their job, know more about how to communicate than you do because they're doing it

every day. And they're people who've been doing it for years. . . .
We often can hurt things by messing with them too much.

John Deford, Product Manager, Colgate

STATE YOUR PROBLEM, NOT THE SOLUTION

Advertisers who get the best advertising from their agencies do not do the agency's job for them. Even though it would have been easier in point six above to have said, "Can't you use a towel in that commercial instead of a diaper?" you could have alienated the creative people. The advertising is their creation. Let them revise it to solve whatever problems you might have so the end result is still their words and visuals even though it also includes your ideas.

DON'T CHANGE FOR THE SAKE OF CHANGE

You may be anxious to see a piece of your thinking in a commercial or print advertisement, but don't change just to make a change to your specifications. As a collaborator, your contributions to the advertising may not always be tangible. Instead, you may have provided the creative inspiration. Let the creative people have the glory and recognition that goes along with creating outstanding advertising. Your glory will come from the increased sales advertising can build. Also know that big ideas are *very* fragile. Sometimes even one change can interrupt the flow of a commercial and diminish its effectiveness.

DON'T SHOW THE ADVERTISING AROUND

It's understandable that you might like to find a supporting viewpoint among your colleagues, friends, or spouse when you feel uncomfortable with advertising, but you'll frustrate your agency team by making them respond to comments from people who are not directly involved. Advertising is a solution to a problem. People who are not privy to the problem cannot properly evaluate the solution.

BE APPRECIATIVE

Even though the creative people are employed by the agency, they are working for you, too. They want you to like the advertising; they want you to run it; and they also want you to understand how hard they have worked to help sell your product. Therefore, show your appreciation. Say thank you. Better yet, write a thank-you note after a major presentation. Many writers and art directors actually save the thank-you notes they receive from clients. A proper sense of appreciation will bring you loyalty, as well as renewed enthusiasm for your company, for your product, and for you.

> I'd like them to know that we like to be appreciated. I had this guy who's the lowest person on the brand . . . and he called me yesterday to tell me that some little five-second insert we'd done in the commercial—that everyone just liked it so much. He called long distance to tell me that. I thought "That is the nicest thing." They probably don't know how much that meant. Hardly anyone does that. You'll put in a call report: "We think it's good work," but the personal element isn't there. . . . This personal gesture is all icing on the cake, but it really does mean a lot.
>
> *A copywriter*

DON'T HESITATE TO ASK FOR MORE
WORK, IF IT'S NEEDED

If, after a full discussion with the agency, you believe that some areas have not been covered or you honestly believe that the agency is capable of creating better advertising than they have shown you, send them back to come up with new ideas. Give solid direction, as you would in a briefing, but also try to inspire the agency to stretch, to create work that is stronger and more exciting.

The best lesson I've learned so far is: Don't stop until you've found it.

A marketing manager, food

MAKE SURE THE ADVERTISING SATISFIES YOU—YOU HAVE TO LIVE WITH IT

There comes a difficult time in every creative exploratory when the advertiser must assume final responsibility for what is presented to his management or what is to run in print or on the air. Therefore, you must feel comfortable that your major concerns have been addressed, whether right or wrong. According to Clarence E. Eldridge, former marketing executive of Campbell Soup Company and General Foods:

> At the same time they [the agency] should recognize that their role is to *recommend*, not to *decide* . . . the client *does have* the last word. It will sometimes happen that the agency's recommendation—especially regarding a creative matter—is right and the client's decision is wrong. *But the client has the inalienable right,* by virtue of his control of the purse, *to be wrong.*[4]

> I tended to be very easy on the agencies . . . especially the creative people. . . . I have since learned that you have to be a lot tougher than I originally was and that perhaps I couldn't always take the point of view that creative people were my friends; sometimes I had to risk alienating them by being very strong in my point of view. . . ."It may win you a Clio, but it's not going to sell my product." That's a hard lesson: how to give them negative feedback as well as positive feedback without stepping on their toes. They should have a lot of latitude, but you have to know when to put on the brakes.
>
> *Mary Seggerman, Senior Product Manager, General Foods*

If there are issues that you feel should be addressed, just stick with it. The first couple of times it's a reaction of getting a bloody nose. And the second time getting another one and getting gunshy and realizing you're not doing your job and going back and doing it again. You run into that a lot, especially with your better creative people, because they've gotten where they are as a function of knowing what they like to do and what's successful and what makes things work and are very opinionated about that, like most of us, and fairly egotistical. It's a question of finding the common ground. . . . But you want to hammer and stay with it. You've got to be prepared to hang in there for the battle. . . . But it does get better and everybody comes back to normal.

A product manager, cigarettes

There comes a time when you just have to say "I appreciate all your comments and thinking, but we're going to do it this way."

Abby Kohnstamm, Director of Industry
Marketing, American Express

GO FOR IT

If you've done your briefing well and have established a collaboration with the agency so that they're doing their best for you, then one day at a creative review, you are going to be presented with a big, exciting idea—one that can send your business through the roof. If you recognize it as a big idea, you may be excited, but more likely you will be frightened, too. The bigger and better the idea, the less chance it's ever been tried before and, therefore, the more uncomfortable you will feel. However, if you want great advertising from your agency, you have to be willing to go out on a limb with them, first to your management and sometimes to the consumer, too. Take comfort in the observation made by Booz • Allen & Hamilton in the 1965 study on advertiser-agency relationships: "The more original the idea, the more controversy it is likely to create."[5]

Once you and the agency have reached agreement on the advertising, your next step before production is to gain approval—either from your management, your lawyers, the networks, or all three. It is a complex process that will be analyzed in detail in the next chapter.

NOTES—CHAPTER 9

1. The *New York Times,* January 12, 1982, p. 21.
2. Booz • Allen & Hamilton, Inc., *Management and Advertising Problems* (New York: Association of National Advertisers, Inc., 1965), p. 53.

3. Ibid., p. 121.
4. Clarence E. Eldridge, *The Role of the Advertising Agency* (New York: Association of National Advertisers, Inc., 1966), p. 5.
5. Booz • Allen & Hamilton, Inc., *op. cit.,* p. 84.

CASE 13.
The Stubborn Agency

YOU ARE: The owner of a small business.
THE PROBLEM: The agency has presented a newspaper advertisement that you basically liked, but with which you had a few small problems and one major concern. The agency went back to their offices and revised all the small problems; however, they have refused to change the visual and have not presented you with an alternative. What should you do?

CASE 14.
The First Copy Review

YOU ARE: An assistant product manager recently promoted from marketing research. Your product is a food imitation that is healthier and less expensive than the food it replaces. There is no product manager on the business; you report directly to the group product manager.
THE PROBLEM: Your product has had a copy problem, and the agency has just completed a large advertising exploratory involving several creative teams and two creative directors. Because of the importance and size of the exploratory, the agency will present their work in an atypical meeting where all advertisers, from assistant product manager to division manager, will be present. You have never reviewed advertising before, and because junior people usually are called upon first to speak at creative reviews, you know that you will be on the spot to make appropriate comments and contributions. How should you handle this situation?

chapter 10

The approval process

Unfortunately, the creation and recognition of a big idea are not the end of your quest for great advertising because standing between the big idea and its exposure to consumers are three large hurdles: legal and regulatory clearance, management approval, and research results. If the creative process is characterized by excitement and anticipation, the approval process, in contrast, is characterized by frustration. Instead of creating advertising, you are protecting the work that has already been created.

Let's review the legal and regulatory hurdle first. In most cases, the advertiser and agency should have begun the clearance process while the advertising was being developed. Sometimes, basic claims are cleared before the agency is briefed. The legal and regulatory hurdle is included here, however, because it is part of the overall approval process.

HOW TO OBTAIN LEGAL AND REGULATORY APPROVAL

Advertising is a highly regulated industry. As a consumer, that is comforting to know. As an advertiser, that means there are many procedures you must follow in order to make certain that the advertising you are about to run is compliant with the many rules and regulations that govern it. These rules and regulations were developed by two primary sources: the government and industry. Although subject to constant change, they form the backbone of advertising regulation.

Government Regulators

Federal Trade Commission. Through the FTC Act of 1914, "unfair or deceptive acts or practices in commerce" are prohibited. The FTC regulates commerce by monitoring advertising and receiving complaints from individual consumers and companies. If its initial investigation of questionable advertising warrants further proceedings, the FTC is empowered to require the presence of advertisers and agencies at hearings, and, after a hearing decision or the negotiation of a settlement, it can impose a cease and desist order. This order delineates the restrictions on future advertising. Violation of the cease and desist order can result in high fines. In one recent case, the court upheld a penalty of $1.7 million against an advertiser.

The FTC Improvements Act of 1975 gave the FTC added enforcement powers. Now the commission can notify Company A of Company B's cease and desist order and hold Company A to the same restrictions. It can sue Company A and impose fines for violating the order even though it was never part of the original proceeding.

Additionally, the Improvements Act confirmed the FTC's power to establish trade regulation rules, which regulate entire industries. The FTC used this authority in the late 1970s to attempt to control the advertising of food, over-the-counter drugs, used cars, funeral homes, and children's cereals and toys. While Congress has not supported the FTC in this area, and most rules have not yet become final, the act does provide that any violation of a *final* rule constitutes an illegal act under the FTC act, subject to fines.

The FTC is empowered to sue on behalf of the public at large and on behalf of individuals. Fines can be as high as $10,000 for each day a commercial airs.

Other federal agencies. Individual industries are often regulated by government agencies and, therefore, the agencies have indirect control over their advertising. The following is a list of major federal agencies and some of the industries they control.

- Securities and Exchange Commission—brokerage firms.
- Federal Communications Commission—broadcasters.
- Bureau of Alcohol, Tobacco & Firearms—alcohol, tobacco, and firearms.

- Food and Drug Administration—labeling of food, drugs, cosmetics, sanitary protection.
- Post Office—all direct-mail advertising, lotteries.

State and local governments. Most states have "little FTC acts" enforced by the state attorneys general. Many municipalities have regulations that expand on the state laws and are enforced by local consumer-protection agencies.

Industry Regulators

The two major industry regulators are the broadcasters—primarily the three large networks, ABC, CBS, and NBC—and business itself, through the National Advertising Division of the Council of Better Business Bureaus.

Broadcast regulation. Under the Federal Communications Commission, which licenses broadcasters, television and radio networks and stations are required to "broadcast in the public interest." This regulation covers advertising as well as program content and includes both "truth in advertising" and "taste and propriety" principles.

The networks and stations are responsible for the advertising they air; therefore, each network and many stations must approve all advertising *in advance* of its being aired. Broadcasters require prior substantiation for all claims made in advertising copy in order to comply with the truth in advertising principle. In questions of taste and propriety, broadcasters have final approval of language and the visuals used. Broadcasters have very strict guidelines on feminine-hygiene advertising and toy or breakfast cereal advertising aimed at children.

Prior to March 1982, the National Association of Broadcasters had a code of advertising principles that served as a general guideline for the networks and some stations. However, because of a suit brought by the Justice Department, the NAB suspended its code, and it has not been reinstated at this writing. Therefore, each network has established its own guidelines.

National Advertising Division of the Council of Better Business Bureaus. The NAD, which also has a code of truth in advertising and taste and propriety principles, monitors all advertising, both print and broadcast. Although it does not pre-clear advertising, as the broadcasters do, it can investigate advertisers and receive complaints from consumers and companies. The NAD is highly respected as an industry self-regulator. Challenges to advertisers and agencies brought by the NAD are most often complied with. Those that are not, can, theoretically, be forwarded to the FTC for action. A list of NAD decisions and agreements is published from time to time in *Advertising Age*.

Areas of Strictest Regulation

Regulation can be more strict for some product areas and some types of advertising executions than for others. If your product appears below, or if you are planning an advertising execution described below, you should thoroughly investigate the applicable regulations. They are far too detailed to cover here.

Products
- Over-the-counter drugs.
- Feminine-hygiene products.
- Toys and cereals advertised to children.
- Beer and wine.
- Tobacco.
- Foods making health claims.

Advertising executions
- Product demonstrations.
- Testimonials—using celebrities, actual users, or *implying* the testimony of actual users (a gray area).
- Comparative advertising.
- Use of a trademark in advertising.

Covering Your Legal and Regulatory Bases

To ensure that your advertising complies with all the rules, regulations, laws, and principles of the government, industry, and the networks—in other words, to stay out of serious and expensive trouble—you should adhere to the following clearance procedure.

First, in product advertising, clear all copy with your research and development department and, if applicable, marketing research as well. In service advertising, clear claims with the most senior person in the area of the claim and, again, marketing research, if applicable. You should obtain clearance as early in the copy-development process as possible. All clearance should be given to you in writing. This documentation will be needed in the next clearance steps. Second, submit all advertising to your company's lawyers along with all documentation. Make certain that the advertising is cleared through your agency's lawyers as well. Comply with any further documentation or releases they require. Third, submit broadcast advertising and substantiation to the three networks or local stations, too, if they require it.

The legal approval process is very time-consuming. If not already available, claim substantiation can take months. Allow at least a week for company and agency legal approvals once you have documentation, and two to three weeks for network clearance.

HOW TO OBTAIN MANAGEMENT APPROVAL

Of the three hurdles, management approval is by far the most frustrating. Of course, if you are the head of your own company and have the final say on advertising, then you do not have to shepherd the advertising through anyone else; but if you are a product manager, you may have anywhere from *two* to *six* more layers of approval before a commercial or print advertisement is produced or tested. That's two to six more *people* each wanting to contribute to the advertising—either to justify their jobs or for the ego gratification of seeing an idea in print or on television. Each person may have his own subjective view, not only about advertising in general, but also about the specific advertising you are presenting. Advertising can be improved as it proceeds through the approval layers, but it can also be diluted and changed beyond recognition.

Advertisers understand that the approval process is often a problem. In a joint study (see Appendix) by the Association of

National Advertisers and the American Association of Advertising Agencies analyzed by William Weilbacher in his book *Auditing Productivity,* 41 percent of advertiser companies responding said that the multilayered approval process "always" or "often" inhibited the productivity of their agency relationships. This was the factor that was singled out more often than any other by advertisers. The implication is that advertisers are well aware that their organizational structures inhibit this productivity, but that they are designed to accomplish other, more important, purposes.[1]

Booz • Allen & Hamilton cited the problem:

> The product management organization often inserts creative judgments at each level of the chain of command. Adjustments and compromises may eliminate or water-down imaginative ideas and contribute to the mediocrity of the end product. Inherent in this process is the continuing frustration of agency creative people.[2]

At the product manager level, the multilayered approval process can produce some defeatism and lowered expectations for the attainment of outstanding advertising.

> The creation of great advertising is further complicated by the fact that there are so many people in the approval process that if something really great is created—and a little oddball comes along—it's very easy for it to get eliminated. Because one person in this incredibly long approval process doesn't like it or feels uncomfortable or says it's a risk. It's why we have so many commercials that use slice-of-life, that are the easiest kind of commercials to get approved.
>
> *A product manager, food*

If advertisers agree that the multilayered approval process is a detriment to outstanding advertising, why does this system persist in so many companies? Two reasons: First, advertiser companies are not organized for the approval of advertising. Most are organized for financial control. The process for most business decisions begins with a lower-level manager making a recommendation, documenting it, and attaching a price tag and/or profit projection. The amount of approval the lower-level manager needs is often determined by the cost and profitability of her proposal. This process works quite well for decisions based on numbers, but in the subjective area of advertising judgment, the original recommendation is often changed or compromised to suit personal tastes and opinions.

The second reason that the multilayered approval process persists is that advertising is as professionally and personally important to upper management as it is to you. As we discussed in Chapter 1, advertising is highly visible. It can be changed more easily, quickly, and at less expense than any other major marketing tool. Therefore, upper management often wants to contribute in order to assume partial credit for any success the advertising creates. They also do not want to take unnecessary risks, because bad or controversial advertising reflects on them as much as outstanding advertising. In a large organization, you will probably have to live with the multilayered approval process. Here's how to proceed through it and emerge with you and the advertising relatively unscathed.

Guidelines for Obtaining Management Approval

Develop a selling strategy with the agency. Selling advertising requires the same kind of strategic thinking and documentation as selling any other business plan. You must develop a recommendation, rationale, and supporting evidence. However, it's more difficult with advertising because, unless you have already tested the advertising, you must work with subjective opinions instead of numbers. Work with your agency to develop your strategy. If they can help sell your product or service to consumers, they can help sell *their* product, the advertising, to your management. Decide with the agency:

- Who will deliver the setup.
- In what order the advertising will be presented.
- What questions management is likely to ask.
- What risks are involved, if any.
- How much detail should be covered.
- Who should make the final recommendation.

Rehearse with the agency. Tell them what you're planning to say. Have them tell you what they plan to say.

Find out all you can about your management's advertising philosophy. Anticipate questions and arguments and be armed with the answers.

Present a united front. If advertiser and agency proceed through management in agreement with each other, they are asking only for approval of that which has already been decided. If, however, they exhibit a difference of opinion, they are really begging for management's involvement in making a decision, which can lead to changes they do not wish to make.

Support your agency. If you have collaborated with your agency for many weeks or months, worked with them to create and revise the advertising to reach total agreement among all collaborators, you owe it to the advertising and the agency to fight your hardest to convince your management to run it. Your support will not only help sell the advertising you are presenting at the moment, but you will also build loyalty and dedication in your long-term advertiser-agency collaboration. The next time the agency creates advertising for you, they will work their hardest because they know they will ultimately have your support.

Of course, it's difficult in the public forum of an advertising meeting to disagree with your boss, to go out on a limb and fight for something about which he is skeptical, but your support can do more to save a big advertising idea than the entire forces of the agency combined because your boss wants to support you. If you simply fold under the pressure, switch your allegiance in a presentation from the agency to your boss, you risk the disrespect of the agency and perhaps your management as well. If you must lose, at least go down fighting.

> Once I have approved the storyboards that are to be presented to my management, I will support the agency one hundred percent. I may have capitulated to the agency on several points, but if, on the whole, I am satisfied with their output, I will not tell my management of any problems I may have had. I go to bat for the agency and am very verbal in my support.
>
> *Mary Seggermann, Senior Product Manager, General Foods*

Presell the advertising.   This does not mean showing the copy. It does mean letting your management know that you've seen some advertising that you believe is strong so that they will be *predisposed* to liking it. You might even consider having your agency help presell it. The management supervisor, in her next conversation with your marketing director, could let him know that some terrific advertising will be presented to him. Certainly preselling the advertising is an obvious tactic, and marketing managers know they are being presold; nevertheless, it usually helps. Preselling creates an atmosphere of anticipation and predisposition to liking—and, therefore, approving—the advertising about to be presented.

Although changes will undoubtedly be made as you present copy up through the layers, you can improve your chances of having the copy emerge to your satisfaction if you follow the preceding guidelines.

TWO CONTROVERSIES: PRESENTING ADVERTISING YOU DON'T LIKE AND SNEAK PREVIEWING THE ADVERTISING

What do you do if the agency wants to present advertising to your management that you think is unacceptable? If you have a good collaborative relationship with your agency, no copy should be totally unacceptable; however, with advertising about which the agency feels strongly, consider the following route.

- Agree to your agency presenting the advertising you don't like. First, they are the advertising experts and respect for them should give them the opportunity to show work in which they believe to a person in your management who may have more experience judging copy than you do. Second, you may be wrong.

The best product managers can say, "Well, I don't agree with you, but I'd like to give you a forum for it and we'll go up the line and not dismiss it out of hand."

A product manager, food

If the agency feels very strongly about a particular campaign that I am uncomfortable with, and if I can't come to a meeting of the minds with the agency, yes, I will let them take it to my manager. I will usually not prejudice my manager ahead of time.

Mary Seggermann, Senior Product Manager, General Foods

- Tell your agency that you will not support them in the meeting. They will have to fight for that particular advertising on their own. There is no reason why you should misrepresent your feelings to your management. You are being fair by giving the agency a forum, but obviously, without your support, the advertising has less of a chance of being approved.
- Your only risk in letting the agency proceed is that your management may see your errors in judgment. If you are wrong and the advertising idea turns out to be great, you wind up with great advertising ultimately succeeding anyway. If you are correct, then your judgment will be recognized by your boss and you will still have maintained a solid relationship with your agency.

A second controversy in the management approval process is sneak previewing. Should you show advertising to your management before the agency presents it? Ninety-eight percent of the time, no! You are robbing the advertising of its best presentation and, therefore, its best chances for approval. For example, a television commercial should not be silently read off a page. It should be heard and acted, because ultimately the consumer will see and hear it on television, not read it. You are also robbing the advertising of its best defense, because the people who can best answer your management's questions about the advertising are not present. Finally, you are robbing the agency of their opportunity to shine in front of the people who hired them, to see a reaction to their copy, which is part of their psychological reward and satisfaction.

No! I will never speak with my management about the advertising before the agency presents. That is not fair. . . . It is their presentation to my manager and it should be done the proper way, the way they would like to present it. To show your manager a storyboard ahead of time is really a mistake—unless you have a very severe philosophical difference with the agency where they refused, which they sometimes do, to do what you wanted them to do. Then you might say to your manager, "The copy you will see tomorrow has not been approved by me." But I would never take away their thunder by going over the copy ahead of time with my manager.

A product manager, food

What are the rare exceptions to the rule that makes sneak previewing permissible? First, if you truly believe that this is the only way to convince your management to approve a specific advertisement. In that case, you might discuss the strategy for the sneak preview with your agency. Second, if one of your managers absolutely insists on seeing the copy before the agency presentation. It happens on occasion, and you may be in a position where it is difficult to say no.

Of course, some product managers or advertising directors do show copy to their management, perhaps to cover themselves or because they are in disagreement with the agency and need support to change or kill a particular advertisement. However, if you have a good collaborative relationship with your agency, you should have worked out all the problems together. Sneak previewing destroys the presentation, destroys a united front, and what can suffer is the integrity and effectiveness of the advertising.

THE TESTING PROCESS

As previously noted (Chapter 8), marketing research is often conducted prior to the development of positioning, strategy, and advertising. Additionally, most companies also use research to measure the effectiveness of their advertising—either in rough or finished form—prior to running it. The reason is obvious: A media budget is often many millions of dollars, and the budget should be spent behind the most effective advertising. Marketing research can help predict the relative effectiveness of advertising alternatives.

(NOTE: Marketing research is an important marketing tool, far too complex to be covered here in detail. If you are not already familiar with the basics of marketing research, you might consider a course or book on the subject.)

There are three primary methods of measuring both print and broadcast advertising: communication, recall, and persuasion. Most testing includes one or a combination of these measurements.

Communications testing.   Communications testing measures whether your advertising is communicating the message you want it to. Although it is only a partial measurement of advertising effectiveness—an advertisement can communicate without being memorable or persuading consumers to try a product or service—communication is extremely important. For example, one product from a major manufacturer failed in test market partly because its advertising described the product as being "aspirin-free" instead of "contains an aspirin substitute." Consumers did not perceive the product as offering pain relief, which was one of its major benefits.

Recall testing.   Recall testing measures the ability of a print or broadcast advertisement to be remembered, usually 24 hours after it was exposed to consumers. For on-air recall, television commercials appear in a regularly scheduled program, and consumers are contacted 24 hours later to determine whether they watched the program and whether they recall the advertising. Print advertisements are usually stripped into a magazine, which is placed in consumers' homes. Consumers are then contacted 24 hours later to determine whether they read the magazine and whether they recall the advertising.

Recall testing is based on the premise that for a consumer to purchase your product or service, she must first be aware of your product or service. Recall of advertising has been positively correlated to awareness. The higher the recall, the greater the awareness the advertising can create of the product or service and its specific benefits.

Persuasion testing. By employing a purchase-intention measurement both before and after exposure to advertising, marketing research can measure the relative persuasion of advertising alternatives. For example, if 10 percent of consumers want to purchase a product before they are exposed to the advertising and 15 percent want to purchase the product after exposure, the advertising receives a pre-post persuasion score of 5.

Each method described above has its own strengths and weaknesses. Most large companies have a preferred method of testing advertising and may even have developed their own methods. However, you should be aware that no research measurement is able to predict perfectly how an advertisement can perform in the marketplace.

Advertising testing can be expensive, ranging from about $2,000 for a simple communications test to $10,000 or more per advertisement for a combination recall and persuasion test. The size of your advertising budget should be your guide for how much to spend on advertising testing.

USING RESEARCH RESULTS

To whichever method you or your company subscribes, how you use the research results is as important as any direction the research might give you. Here are three guidelines.

Decide before testing how the results are to be evaluated. What score must the advertising attain to be acceptable for running? Which copy point should be recalled at the highest level? To set an "action standard" for your advertising, you might compare the results to those for your competitors or to those for previous commercials for your product or service. Most testing services have norms by which to judge advertising results.

Use research to help you reach a decision, not to make the decision for you. Research is not intended to replace judgment, only to aid it. According to Ronald Leong, group product manager at Bristol-Myers,

I don't think you can find anyone who will apply one hundred percent reliability to any advertising testing that's ever been developed by any company or agency. . . . I think that's a mistake a lot of people make. They use research as a crutch. The whole business is subjective. . . . What you have to do is apply as much input, particularly facts and information, as you can to help focus on reducing the risk and take all that and make a judgment.

Advertising testing is far from perfect. Often it can only reflect the factual points made in a commercial, not the emotion created for the product or service being advertised. Sometimes emotion can be more effective in selling than a copy claim. Perfume or cosmetic advertising is a good example.

Sometimes, too, when a group of commercials is tested, results can be very close and judgment must be used to decide which commercial to air. For example, for one product with unique product features, four introductory commercials were tested. The commercial selected had neither the highest persuasion nor the highest recall score, but it did have the highest recall of its unusual product features. Agency and advertiser agreed that this commercial would create the highest awareness of product uniqueness and, therefore, in the long run, would be the strongest.

Collaborate with your agency in interpreting research results. Try not to use research results to make changes that could boost recall of one copy point but hamper the overall effectiveness of the commercial.

Agencies often accuse advertisers of interpreting results too literally, of sacrificing a human element to stress a factual one. Advertisers often accuse agencies of resisting research direction. Just remember that until an advertisement is placed on the air or in a publication, it is still in the process of being created, and collaboration is still the most effective way to produce the most effective advertising.

After testing results have been obtained, you may want to re-present the advertising to your management to show them the changes you and the agency have made. The same procedures apply when presenting revised advertising as when you presented initially: Formulate a selling strategy with the agency;

present a united front; support the agency; presell, if necessary. With final management approval, you are ready to produce finished advertising for broadcast or print media.

NOTES—CHAPTER 10

1. William M. Weilbacher, *Auditing Productivity* (New York: Association of National Advertisers, Inc., 1981), p. 38.
2. Booz • Allen & Hamilton, Inc., *Management & Advertising Problems* (New York: Association of National Advertisers, Inc., 1965), p. 52.

chapter 11

An introduction
to broadcast production

At the production stage of a television or radio commercial, the circle of collaborators is widened to include the dozens of people whose expertise is needed to make a television storyboard or radio script come alive. In television you must work with a director, camera operator, actors, editor, electricians, prop people, stylists, makeup people, and sound engineers, to name a few. In radio, the cast of collaborators is smaller but still includes engineers, actors, and, if music is required, composers, musicians, and singers.

It is probably more difficult for the advertiser to contribute at the production stage than at other stages of the creative process because marketing expertise is not related to the expertise needed to produce an outstanding commercial. Nevertheless, as the advertiser, you are still responsible for the final advertising product and, therefore, want to understand the complete production process. This chapter will give you production basics so you will feel more comfortable as the production process proceeds, and so that you can communicate your comments in terms that will be readily understood.

Before we discuss the production process, here are two important pieces of advice: *Plan your production far enough in advance* so that you use time and equipment most efficiently and so you don't have to go into overtime. In production, time equals money. Overtime can mean double or even triple time. Second, *speak up early* if you have a problem. It's easier and less expensive to change a word on a storyboard than it is to reshoot or rerecord. It's easier to choose a different take (reading of a scene) at the rough-cut stage than it is after the optical is made.

TELEVISION PRODUCTION

Television Commercial Production Costs

Television commercials can cost from $10,000 to over $1 million depending on the complexity of the commercial, how many people are in it, and many other variables. According to *Marketing and Media Decisions* magazine, television commercials cost 5.5 times as much per minute as the average made-for-television movie and about 50 percent more than the average-minute cost of many theatrical films.[1] However, although commercial production is expensive and costs must be scrutinized, commercial production is not a time to scrimp, either. You should look at the cost of your television production in relationship to your overall media budget. A commercial that costs $50,000 to $90,000 may still be less than 5 percent of a $2.5 million media budget. When an advertiser is spending millions on advertising, he should make certain that his product or service is shown to its best advantage in the commercial.

If you have a limited budget for commercial production, you should have told your agency at their briefing. A commercial that was created to have a large cast, complex sets, or to be shot on many locations cannot be produced inexpensively and still be good, effective advertising. However, if a budget does exist before the creative process exists, the creative team can work within those guidelines. Perhaps a less expensive commercial without a set and with a single actor talking to the camera won't be as effective as a more elaborate commercial, but then again, it might be. It all depends on the product or service, the strategy, and the creative idea. Three major factors affect commercial production costs. Let's review them.

Production people. Production crews are usually unionized, and their costs are fixed. A specific number of people are required if sound equipment is to be used, if the commercial is to be shot on location, if sets are to be built, and so on. A location crew can average 20 people, not counting the director and camera operator.

Directors.   Directors' fees can vary from $3,000 to as high as $15,000 for a director with a particular specialty, such as sports, musicals, or spectacular locations. A director is as important to the production of a commercial as he is to the production of a feature film. He will be selected by the advertising agency for his expertise with a particular type of commercial—be it slice-of-life, testimonials, humor, food, sports. It is his vision of how the storyboard will be translated to film or tape that makes the commercial come alive.

Talent.   Virtually all actors and actresses used in commercial production are union members, and their base payments are fixed. Actors receiving scale or double scale will work within a standard union contract. Special contracts with negotiated fees and guarantees are used only for "star" talent, such as film, stage, or sports personalities.

"Star" talent costs are negotiated, and this should be done up front. Contract-renewal terms should also be negotiated before the "star" is signed. Costs can be scaled according to how the commercial will be used: one fee for shooting and testing the commercial, an additional fee if the commercial is used in test markets, and a final fee if the commercial is used nationally. Often the head of the agency's casting department is responsible for the tricky task of negotiating star contracts.

In addition to a fee for the day(s) of production, talent is also paid residuals, fees for every time the commercial is aired. Residuals are set in 13-week cycles, and the fees for the day(s) of production are applied to the first cycle. Unless the advertiser does not plan to air the commercial in the future, talent is paid a holding fee for all additional cycles of 13 weeks, whether or not the commercial is aired during the cycle. If it is aired, the holding fee is applied against the residuals.

The amount of the residuals is determined by whether the commercial is running on national network television or in spot markets. Network residuals are higher because of the vast audience reached. Spot residuals are scaled to the size of the market. New York and Los Angeles are more expensive than Baltimore or Peoria.

Other factors affecting commercial costs. There are some areas that affect costs more than others. They include multiple-location shooting; overtime shooting (nights, weekends); elaborate sets, which must be constructed and taken down, adding the cost of both labor and materials; and special visual effects, which may require special opticals or the use of computer-generated pictures.

Rough Production

When an advertiser wants to test several executions to determine which is the most effective to place on the air, commercials are often produced in rough form first. Although rough production cannot have all of the commercial values and impact of finished production, it can communicate the basic selling message of the commercial and be measured relative to other commercials for communication, recall, and/or persuasion.

There are three basic forms of rough production. You should work with your agency to determine which form will best convey the essentials of the commercial at the least possible cost. Rough production costs vary enormously depending on precisely how rough the commercial is and where in the United States it is being made. In New York City, an animatic with few drawings, few camera moves, and rough voice recording can be made for as little as $3,000. The three types of rough production are as follows:

> *Animatic*—a series of illustrations, filmed with some camera moves plus a voice or music track.
>
> *Photomatic*—similar to an animatic except that photographs are substituted for illustrations. Unless scrap photos are used, photomatics can be as expensive as livomatics.
>
> *Livomatic*—shot in a studio with an actor or actors standing in front of a photograph of the set or location. The set is lit simply, and 16mm film or tape is used in the production. Also, an inexpensive director who may specialize in test commercials is used.

Preproduction

If a commercial production is to proceed smoothly and effectively, a great deal of planning must take place before the camera rolls. The agency producer coordinates preproduction as well as production and postproduction. After she receives approved storyboards from the account group, her next job is to obtain bids from commercial production houses. She will discuss the choice of director with the creative team; when they have narrowed the choice down to three houses, she will invite them to bid on the boards. This three-bid system is frequently used to obtain the lowest prices for the advertiser, but some companies do bid fewer than three houses or have some other arrangement. You should check within your company to learn the rules of commercial bidding. You should also ask for a "ballpark" production cost when commercials are presented to you.

When a commercial production house estimates costs, it will often follow the form from the Association of Independent Commercial Producers. It includes virtually every cost involved in producing a commercial. This form is on pages 147 through 152.

Once the bids are received, the agency will review them with you and present a recommendation. Sometimes the recommendation may not be the lowest bid, especially if it includes using a director who the agency believes is worth an additional expense. When you review the estimates, ask questions. You may not be able to reduce the costs, but at least you will understand them. If you are about to be involved in your first commercial production, try to review the estimate with the agency producer as well as the account executive. You may learn more about production that way.

Casting

While the estimating process is getting started, the agency will also have initiated casting for the commercial. This includes preparation of casting specifications, usually a profile of the type of people to be used in the commercial, including age, physical description, type of personality. *You should approve the casting specifications before casting is begun.* Casting also includes au-

FILM PRODUCTION COST SUMMARY

	Bid Date	Actualization Date	
Production Co.:	Agency:	Agency job #	
Address:	Client:	Product:	
Telephone No.: Job #			
Production Contact:	Agency prod:	Tel:	
Director:	Agency art dir:	Tel:	
Cameraman:	Agency writer:	Tel:	
Set Designer:	Agency Bus. Mgr.:	Tel:	
Editor:	Commercial title: No.: Length:		
No. pre-prod. days pre-light/rehearse	1.		
No. build/strike days Hours:	2.		
No. Studio shoot days Hours:	3.		
No. Location days Hours:	4.		
Location sites:	5.		
	6.		

SUMMARY OF ESTIMATED PRODUCTION COSTS		ESTIMATED	ACTUAL		
1. Pre-production and wrap costs	Totals A & C				
2. Shooting crew labor	Total B				
3. Location and travel expenses	Total D				
4. Props, wardrobe, animals	Total E				
5. Studio & Set Construction Costs	Totals F, G, and H				
6. Equipment costs	Total I				
7. Film stock develop and print: No. feet mm Total J					
8. Miscellaneous	Total K				
9.	Sub-Total: A to K				
10. Director/creative fees (Not Included In Direct Cost) Total L					
11. Insurance					
12.	Sub-Total: Direct Costs				
13. Production Fee					
14. Talent costs and expenses	Totals M and N				
15. Editorial and finishing per:					
16.					
17.	Grand Total (Including Director's Fee)				
18. Contingency					

Comments:

PAGE 1

A: PRE-PRO/WRAP   **B: SHOOT**

	CREW	ESTIMATED				ACTUAL					ESTIMATED				ACTUAL			
		Days	Rate	O/T Hrs	Total	Days	Rate	O/T $	Total		Days	Rate	O/T Hrs	Total	Days	Rate	O/T $	Total
1	Producer:									51								
2	Assistant Director:									52								
3	Director Photography:									53								
4	Camera Operator:									54								
5	Asst. Cameraman:									55								
6	Outside Prop:									56								
7										57								
8	Inside Prop:									58								
9										59								
10										60								
11	Electrician:									61								
12										62								
13										63								
14										64								
15										65								
16	Grip:									66								
17										67								
18										68								
19										69								
20	Mixer:									70								
21	Boom Man:									71								
22	Recordist:									72								
23	Playback:									73								
24	Make-Up:									74								
25	Hair:									75								
26	Stylist:									76								
27	Wardrobe Attendant:									77								
28	Script Clerk:									78								
29	Home Economist:									79								
30	Asst. Home Economist:									80								
31	VTR Man:									81								
32	EFX Man:									82								
33	Scenic:									83								
34	Telepr. Operator:									84								
35	Generator Man:									85								
36	Still Man:									86								
37	Loc. Contact/Scout:									87								
38	P.A.									88								
39	2nd A.D.									89								
40	Nurse:									90								
41	Craft Service:									91								
42	Fireman:									92								
43	Policeman:									93								
44	Wlfr./Tchr.:									94								
45	Teamster									95								
46										96								
47										97								
48										98								
49										99								
50										100								

Sub Total A			Sub Total B	
PT/P & W			PT/P & W	
TOTAL A			**TOTAL B**	

PAGE 2

PRE-PRODUCTION & WRAP/MATERIALS & EXPENSES	ESTIMATED	ACTUAL	
101. Auto Rentals (No. of Cars)			
102. Air Fares: No. of people ( ) x Amount per fare ( )			
103. Per Diems: No. of people ( ) x Amount per day ( )			
104. Still Camera Rental & Film			
105. Messengers			
106. Trucking			
107. Deliveries & Taxis			
108. Home Economist Supplies			
109. Telephone & Cable			
110. Casting Call/Prep_____ Days Casting_____Days Call Back_____Days			
111. Casting Facilities			
112. Working Meals			
113.			
Sub Total C			

LOCATION EXPENSES	ESTIMATED	ACTUAL	
114. Location Fees			
115. Permits			
116. Car Rentals			
117. Bus Rentals			
118. Camper Dressing Room Vehicles			
119. Parking, Tolls, & Gas			
120. Trucking			
121. Other vehicles			
122. Other vehicles			
123. Customs			
124. Air freight/ Excess baggage			
125. Air Fares: No. of people ( ) x cost per fare ( )			
126. Per Diems: Total No. man days ( ) x amt. per day ( )			
127. Air fares: No. of people ( ) x cost per fare ( )			
128. Per Diems: Total No. man days ( ) x amt. per day ( )			
129. Breakfast: No. of man days ( ) x amt. per person ( )			
130. Lunch: No. of man days ( ) x amt. per person ( )			
131. Dinner: No. of man days ( ) x amt. per person ( )			
132. Guards			
133. Limousines (Celebrity Service)			
134. Cabs and Other Transportation			
135. Kit Rental			
136. Art Work			
137. Gratuities			
138.			
139.			
Sub Total D			

PROPS AND WARDROBE & ANIMALS	ESTIMATED	ACTUAL	
140. Prop Rental			
141. Prop Purchase			
142. Wardrobe Rental			
143. Wardrobe Purchase			
144. Picture Vehicles			
145. Animals & Handlers			
146. Wigs & Mustaches			
147. Color Correction			
148.			
149.			
150.			
Sub Total E			

PAGE 3

STUDIO RENTAL & EXPENSES—STAGE	ESTIMATED				ACTUAL			
	Days	Hrs	Rate	Total	Days	Hrs	Rate	Total
151. Rental for Build Days								
152. Rental for Build O.T. Hours								
153. Rental for Pre-Lite Days								
154. Rental for Pre-Lite O.T. Hours								
155. Rental for Shoot Days								
156. Rental for Shoot O.T. Hours								
157. Rental for Strike Days								
158. Rental for Strike O.T. Hours								
159. Generator & Operator								
160. Set Guards								
161. Total Power Charge & Bulbs								
162. Misc. Studio Charges (Cartage, Phone, Coffee)								
163. Meals for Crew & Talent (Lunch, Dinner)								
164.								
165.								
166.								
167.								
Sub Total F								

SET CONSTRUCTION (CREW FOR BUILD, STRIKE, PRELIGHT)	ESTIMATED				ACTUAL			
	Days	Rate	O/T Hrs.	Total	Days	Rate	O/T $	Total
168. Set Designer Name:								
169. Carpenters								
170. Grips								
171. Outside Props								
172. Inside Props								
173. Scenics								
174. Electricians								
175. Teamsters								
176. Men for Strike								
177. P.A.s								
178.								
179.								
180.								
		Sub Total G						
		PT/P & W						
		TOTAL G						

SET CONSTRUCTION MATERIALS	ESTIMATED	ACTUAL	
181. Props (Set Dressing Purchase)			
182. Props (Set Dressing Rental)			
183. Lumber			
184. Paint			
185. Hardware			
186. Special Effects			
187. Special Outside Construction			
188. Trucking			
189. Messengers/Deliveries			
190. Kit Rental			
191.			
192.			
Sub Total H			

PAGE 4

EQUIPMENT RENTAL	ESTIMATED	ACTUAL	
193. Camera Rental			
194. Sound Rental			
195. Lighting Rental			
196. Grip Rental			
197. Generator Rental			
198. Crane/Cherry Picker Rental			
199. VTR Rental With Playback _____ Without Playback _____			
200. Walkie Talkies, Bull Horns			
201. Dolly Rental			
202. Camera Car			
203. Helicopter			
204. Production Supplies			
205. Teleprompter			
206.			
207.			
208.			
209.			
210..			
Sub Total I			

FILM RAW STOCK DEVELOP AND PRINT	ESTIMATED			ACTUAL		
	FOOTAGE	COST/FT.	TOTAL	FOOTAGE	COST/FT.	TOTAL
211. Purchase of raw stock: Footage amount						
212. Developing footage amount						
213. Printing footage amount						
214. Transfer to Mag.						
215. Sync/Screen Dailies						
216.						
Sub Total J						

MISCELLANEOUS COSTS	ESTIMATED	ACTUAL	
217. Petty Cash			
218. Air Shipping/Special Carriers			
219. Phones and Cables			
220. Accountable Cash Expenditures Under $15 Each			
221. External Billing Costs (Computer Accounting, etc.)			
222. Special Insurance			
223.			
224.			
225.			
226.			
Sub Total K			

DIRECTOR/CREATIVE FEES	ESTIMATED	ACTUAL	
227. Prep			
228. Travel			
229. Shoot Days			
230. Post-production			
231.			
232.			
233.			
Sub Total L			

PAGE 5

TALENT	No.	Rate	Days	TRAVEL DAYS	O/T Hrs 1½ X / 2 X	ESTIMATED	No.	Days	ACTUAL
234. O/C Principals									
235. O/C Principals									
236. O/C Principals									
237. O/C Principals									
238. O/C Principals									
239. O/C Principals									
240. O/C Principals									
241. O/C Principals									
242. O/C Principals									
243. O/C Principals									
244.									
245.									
246.									
247. General Extras									
248. General Extras									
249. General Extras									
250. General Extras									
251. General Extras									
252. General Extras									
253.									
254.									
255.									
256. Hand Model									
257.									
258.									
259. Voice Over									
260. Fitting Fees: S.A.G.									
261. Fitting Fees: C.C.C.									
262.									
263. Audition Fees: S.A.G.									
264. Audition Fees: S.E.G.									
265.									
Sub Total									
266. Payroll & P&W Taxes									
267. Wardrobe Allowance: No. of talent ( ) x No. of garments ( ) x fee per garment ( ).									
268.									
Sub Total									
269. Other									
270. Mark-up									
				Sub Total M					

TALENT EXPENSES	ESTIMATED	ACTUAL	
271. Per diem: No. of man days ( ) x amount per day ( )			
272. Air fare: No. of people ( ) x amount per fare ( )			
273. Cabs and other transportation			
274. Mark-Up			
275.			
276.			
Sub Total N			

ditions. Talent comes to the agency or production company and reads for the part(s) in the commercial. Often they will be videotaped so that creative, account, and advertiser can review the casting repeatedly without having the talent return.

Once the agency and director have selected a recommendation, they will present the casting to you for your approval. Once again, you are dealing with a very subjective area—even more subjective than commercial approval because there are no rules at all. Therefore, again, you must trust your instincts. Is the casting believable, convincing? Does the individual fit the specifications agreed to? Do you feel yourself respond as the actor is reading? You may agree with the agency's recommendation or you may simply not really know who is best. If you cannot make a judgment and feel no negatives about the casting recommendations, follow your agency's advice. They have seen a large amount of talent and have expertise in determining who can or can't perform as required and who can or can't cut through the clutter of commercials on television to make the viewer pay attention.

Prep Time

To prepare for production, the production house and agency need approximately two weeks between the time the bid is awarded and the commercial will be shot. During this time, in addition to casting the commercial, the production house and agency must hire the camera operator, design and build a set or scout a location, obtain wardrobe and props, color-correct product packaging, obtain the product. In sum, every aspect of the commercial must be coordinated so that it can be discussed with you at the preproduction meeting.

The Preproduction Meeting

Because commercials are so expensive and time on production day is so valuable, all details of the final production are determined at the preproduction meeting. It is extremely important that you attend. The preproduction meeting brings together all the people who are involved with making a storyboard on paper into an effective film or tape. Attending the meeting is the director, the production-company producer, the creative team, account group, agency producer, and you. Other people may attend also, depending on the commercial. If a demonstration is involved, the agency lawyers may be needed to make certain that the product and demonstration are shot to legal specifications. If the commercial involves food, a home economist may attend. For a fashion or cosmetic commercial, the stylist and makeup man may attend. Everyone involved in the major elements of the final production should attend the preproduction meeting.

The agenda of the meeting may be long. It should cover:

- Legal clearance—Have all clearances been obtained? Are there any scenes or words that need any special attention? Must any special clearance or affidavits be signed? If the commercial involves a demonstration, must it be performed and filmed in any special way so that if questioned by one of the regulatory bodies, it can be substantiated?
- Timing—Is the commercial too long or too short? It should have been timed before it was presented to you; however, it should be double-checked by the director to make certain that any camera or talent moves he has planned will work with the timing already estimated. If copy must be cut, it is far better to do it at the preproduction meeting than on the set after the actors have memorized their lines.
- The set or location—How will the set or location look? Where will the camera be placed? What props, if any, will be added?
- Wardrobe—What will the talent wear?
- The product—If the commercial is for a product, how much is needed? When and where should it be delivered? You, the advertiser, are responsible for obtaining the product and delivering it to the production house. Does the product behave differently under hot lights? Does it need special refrigeration or special cooking? For example, margarine melts quickly when being photographed. Many samples of the product are needed and they must be kept under refrigeration. All the people involved in commercial production will look to your expertise for guidance on how the product performs.
- Casting—Approved casting will be reviewed at the preproduction meeting.
- Direction—Both camera angles and reading of the copy should be covered at the meeting. Where will the camera

be? Close up? Medium shots? If there are two people in the commercial, will they be shot separately, together, or both? How will the talent read the lines? What is their attitude? Is there a range of readings to be covered? What is it?

- Editing—How do the agency and director expect the commercial to be edited? Where do they see cuts? Where dissolves? Do not hold them to a final edit, but you and they should have a good idea of how the commercial will be edited.
- Eliminating alternate versions—From time to time agency and advertiser do not reach agreement on the final script and, in the hope of speeding the creative-approval process, agree to postpone a final decision until after the commercial is shot two or more ways. However, every effort should be made to reach agreement on one version before production begins; sometimes this agreement can be reached at the preproduction meeting. Alternate versions add time, confusion, and cost to a commercial production. Often, seeing a version on film does not make the decision any easier. If you want your director and talent to concentrate and do their best for you, narrow the options before production.
- Production schedule—In addition to the date(s) of production, the agency should also provide a schedule for each stage of postproduction so that you and your management know when you will have to give approvals and when the final commercial will be ready to ship to the stations.

Your function at the preproduction meeting is to understand every point being made and to voice any concerns you might have. In other words, *speak up quickly and often.* If you disagree with the production plans, the agency and director need to understand your reasoning, and you theirs. Once again, you are collaborating and all the rules of collaboration—respect, trust, expertise—apply. If you do not speak up at the preproduction meeting, changes may have to be made on the set. This could be costly and confusing to the director and actors. Again, the earlier in the production process you voice your concerns or suggestions, the better.

Production

The production of a commercial is always exciting, even though it can be slow and tedious, with endless time spent on lighting and numerous readings of the same words. To be effective on the set, you need to understand that commercial-production shoots have their own culture, almost like a foreign country. There is a separate language and a proper way to behave on the set. Some examples of the language are:

"Bells"—warning bells that signal everyone inside and outside the studio to be quiet because sound is about to be recorded.

"Speed"—a word signal from the sound man to the camera operator that the tape recorder is rolling at the proper speed and the action can begin.

"Sticks"—the clapboard that synchronizes the start of a scene both on the film and sound track.

"Action"—the director's direction to the actors to begin the scene.

"Cut"—the director's cue to end the scene.

"Print"—the director's instructions to develop the film of that take. If the take has not been good, it will not be printed, so that money will not be wasted.

"Wrap"—the director's cue that commercial production is finished.

Because there are so many people involved in a commercial production, so much equipment and, therefore, so much money, there is a definite procedure followed on the set to keep the production running smoothly. Your behavior should follow that procedure.

The director is in charge of everyone in the commercial production. He is the boss of the set. *He alone* gives direction to the actors, the camera operator, and, directly or indirectly, to the crew. The agency producer is the liaison with the director. Any comments on readings, the set, the product, from the creative team or the account group should be made to the agency producer, not the director. The agency producer can answer any questions or comments and leave the director to do what he was hired to do: direct!

Your comments, questions, or direction should be given to your account person. If you both agree that some new direction should be given to the actors or that other changes need to be made, the account person will involve the agency producer, who will speak with the director. If you think something is wrong, speak up, but give the actors and director a chance to make the scene flow their way before you interject your opinions. The first few takes of any scene are rehearsals for the actors, director, and camera operator, like a first draft of your marketing plan. Give them a chance to get it right before you comment. Most often, they are feeling the same concerns you are and will work to correct them. Of course, it can be difficult to feel you're contributing when all you're actually doing is watching, but on a shoot your role is more supervisory than contributory. At the best, smoothest shoots, you won't have to say one word!

The unwritten rule of any commercial production is that the commercial must be filmed *as boarded.* While ideas to improve the commercial often evolve at a shoot—new lines, new angles— these can be shot, too, but the commercial must also be filmed as boarded and approved by your management. Most professionals understand this, but in the excitement of production, they may need an occasional reminder. That is the job of the account group and you. Remember, once the director says "Wrap," it will cost a lot of money to go back and reshoot.

Video Tape Recorder (VTR)

As your commercial is being shot, you will be able to see each scene on a television set. You will also be able to play back a tape to determine any changes that might be necessary before moving on to the next scene.

Tape Versus Film

The decision to use tape or film is a creative one to be made by your agency creative team and the producer. Both tape and film have advantages: Tape lends a real, "live" quality to the commercial. It has the advantages of speed in postproduction. Some film commercials are actually "finished" on tape. Film offers advantages of deeper color and texture and more options at the optical stage. In the early stages of postproduction, it is very easy to edit.

Your agency producer will explain the choice of tape versus film to you for the specific commercial(s) you are producing.

POSTPRODUCTION

Postproduction can be divided into three stages ranging from rough to finished production. Your approval will be sought for one or more of the stages, depending on how finished the commercial needs to be before you can envision how it will look finally. For some commercials, you will be involved in all three stages.

Stage 1—The Rough Cut

This is your first chance to see the commercial. It is now in two pieces, video and audio. The video track shows a rough edit of the commercial. (On film, the scenes are literally spliced together by hand.) The video includes no opticals—dissolves, supers, special effects—and no color correction. The audio track includes all the words spoken at the shoot plus the words of the voice-over announcer(s), who will have been recorded after the shoot. The audio track is not mixed. That means the voices from the shoot do not match the level of the voice-over announcer(s), and the backgrounds do not match.

If you have any suggested changes, the rough-cut stage is the time to voice them. Do you agree with the takes chosen? Do you agree with the announcer's intonation? Scenes can easily be reedited at the rough-cut stage and at the least cost.

When you give creative comments at the rough-cut screening, the same rules described in Chapter 9 apply. A creative person is showing you her work, only this time it is the producer instead of the copywriter and art director. Remember to react as a person. Make general comments first. Be sensitive to your creative people. Be honest. Take your time—ask to see the rough cut as often as necessary to help form your opinions. Give reasons for your comments. Don't nitpick. State your problem, not the solution. Don't change for the sake of change. Be appreciative. Make sure *you* are satisfied.

Stage 2—Finishing on Tape

Both commercials shot on film and tape are finished and made color perfect by transferring to tape. Opticals are inserted, audio tracks are mixed, and the commercial is finished at this stage. Your final approval, and that of your management, if they have not seen the commercial before, will be obtained before duplicate tapes are made and shipped to the stations. Shipping is the final step in television production.

RADIO

Radio commercial production is far less complex than television production. In fact, on occasion, it may not exist at all! If a simple commercial with no music or sound effects is read live by a radio station announcer, all the agency needs to do is forward the scripts to the stations. Normally, however, even simple, one-voice commercials are cast and recorded in a studio so that precisely the right voice is used and precisely the right reading is obtained.

Studio recording time costs about $170 to $325 an hour in New York City. That, plus talent, is your only production cost. The basic cost for a voice-over announcer for a radio commercial is $125 plus residuals. Radio commercials can, of course, be more complex than one voice, in which case they will cost more. Factors adding cost include additional actors, special sound effects, music—which will involve a creative fee to the composer as well as talent fees and residuals to all the musicians and singers.

The agency producer usually acts as director for radio commercials. She will run the recording session. Should you choose to attend, the same rules apply as on a television set: Speak up . . . but wait until the producer and actors have rehearsed before you do. At a music recording session, the music composer is in charge. There will be little you can contribute. So just sit back and enjoy seeing how the musical pieces come together.

(A word about music—if you are using it for either a radio or television commercial, a melody line should be presented to you for your approval prior to the music-recording session. Often, composers will charge one fee to create the music, then add a larger fee if their melody is used. That way, you can choose from a variety of melodies at a relatively reasonable cost.)

A radio commercial is usually mixed and recorded at the same studio session. A finished commercial will be presented to you; however, you can still suggest changes and make them at a reasonable cost.

Once approved, the radio commercial will be duplicated and shipped to the stations, and the radio production process is complete.

NOTE—CHAPTER 11

1. Charles Sinclair, "How to Control Commercial Costs on TV," *Marketing and Media Decisions,* Fall 1982, p. 93.

chapter 12

An introduction to print production

At the production stage of a magazine or newspaper advertisement, the circle of collaborators is once again widened to include all the artists and craftsmen whose expertise is needed to translate a layout into a finished advertisement. They include a photographer or illustrator, models, retouchers, typesetters, engravers, and perhaps home economists, stylists, and makeup artists. Although your guidance may be sought during a photography session, your major contributions will be made during the preproduction of the advertisement. To have print production proceed as smoothly as possible, you should follow the same two rules we discussed in the previous chapter: *Plan ahead* because time equals money, and *speak up early*. The further along you are in the production process, the more it costs to make changes.

MAGAZINE PRODUCTION

Magazine production costs can vary enormously—from $1,500 to $50,000 or more. The two factors that do most to determine the cost of a magazine advertisement are the use of color and the number of photographs or illustrations in the advertisement. Color photography can often be more costly than black-and-white, and color engraving is from 6 to 10 times as expensive as black-and-white engraving. Naturally, the cost of photography and engraving is multiplied by the number of photographs in the advertisement. Let's review the four areas that assume the majority of expenses in print production.

Photography or illustration. Selecting a photographer or illustrator is similar to selecting a director for a television commercial. Each has his own style and specialty, such as food, people, or still lifes. The leading, most experienced commercial photographers in New York City can charge as much as $5,000 per color photograph; however, younger men and women and other competent photographers may charge as little as $750. Costs are often negotiable; as in television production, it is wise to obtain three bids. Illustration, or line art, can be somewhat less expensive than photography. However, selecting illustration rather than photography to communicate the selling message is a creative decision, not a cost decision.

How the photograph or illustration will be used in the media also affects its cost. For example, a photograph for a national-magazine advertisement is more expensive than one for local-newspaper use. Specific uses are included in the agreement with the photographer or illustrator, and any additional uses will entail additional costs.

Talent for print advertisements sometimes receive residuals. There are no fixed rules. Residuals depend on the model and the product or service being advertised. However, most contracts do stipulate specific use of the photograph and the length of time it can be used.

Retouching.   No matter how perfect the photograph, it will almost always require some retouching to remove an unwanted shadow or reflection, perhaps to add some tone or color. For black-and-white photography, retouching will be done on a print. For color, minimal retouching can be applied directly to a large transparency. If extensive retouching is required, a special color print called a dye transfer must be made, and retouching will be applied to that instead of to the transparency. Retouching can also be done electronically. Naturally the amount of retouching necessary determines its cost. Your agency may estimate anywhere from a few hundred to a few thousand dollars.

Typography.   Typography costs depend on the amount of copy in the advertisement. Costs can be kept down by limiting the number of times the type must be reset and not setting on overtime. You should try to make all copy changes before the type is set. However, even with perfect planning, type may have to be reset to fit around photographs or to add or subtract words to make the type fit the page better.

Engraving. Engraving is expensive. A black-and-white engraving costs between $500 and $1,200, depending on size. The cost of color engraving depends on the engraving process being used by the publications in which your advertisement will run and ranges from $3,000 to $5,000 *per photograph.*

There are two major forms of engraving used by most magazines: rotogravure (or roto) and lithography, also known as offset. Roto offers higher-quality reproduction and is more expensive. Offset is faster to print, and is used by many weekly publications. Media schedules that include several magazines often require two sets of plates: one for roto and one for offset. However, if just one magazine in your schedule requires roto, you might see whether it can be substituted with a magazine that uses the same offset plates as your other publications. You could save money. Another way to save money is to make one-size advertisement fit all publications. Although all magazines are not the same size, they are often within a quarter of an inch of each other in length and/or width, so you could produce only one engraving for all publications.

The Seven Steps of Print Production

1. Preproduction. The agency should schedule a print-preproduction meeting if you are about to produce a complex or expensive advertisement. Otherwise, the meeting can take the form of a telephone discussion between you and your account executive. Before producing an advertisement, you should have legally approved copy and artwork. Any legal requirements for the photography must be understood—particularly if you are photographing a demonstration or showing the effects of the product in use. For example, a T-shirt in a detergent advertisement must be washed in the detergent before being photographed. Wardrobe must be determined. Models must be selected. (Casting in a print advertisement usually takes the form of reviewing photographs of the models rather than taped auditions.) You must also sign a production estimate before any production work is begun. (See sample on page 164.)

2. Photography or illustration. Once preproduction is complete, the photograph(s) will be taken or the illustrator will

---

Sample Print-Production Estimate

Client/Product _____*Date* _____ *Job #* ____

Layout	_____
Photography	_____
Art	_____
Model Fee	_____
Props	_____
Wardrobe	_____
Dye Transfer	_____
B/W Prints	_____
Retouching	_____
Photostats	_____
Mechanical	_____
Process Lettering	_____
Typography	_____
Engraving	_____
Duplicate Material	_____
Reprints	_____
Printing	_____
Net Total	_____
Agency Commission	_____
Subtotal	_____
Sales Tax	_____
Grand Total	_____
Contingency (10 percent)	_____

---

be commissioned. You may wish to attend the photography session. If you have never attended one, you certainly should go. However, unless the shoot is complicated, your presence will not be needed; even with more complex photography, some advertisers often delegate full responsibility to their agency. The final decision is up to you and your account group.

3. Typesetting.   This step is often initiated simultaneously with the photography. You will not be involved unless copy needs to be edited to fit the layout. Changes should be minor.

4. Retouching.   The decision to retouch is made by the art director. You will not be involved unless your product has specific legal requirements. Again, a demonstration would have the most legal requirements. Obviously, retouching cannot change the results of a demonstration.

5. *Artwork and mechanical.* The first time you see the advertisement, it will be in at least two pieces. You will be presented with the retouched artwork or illustrations and the mechanical, a guide for the positioning of all parts of the advertisement—the type, artwork, logo. Your approval is required before engraving. Remember that engraving is extremely expensive; therefore, you should make any changes when you see the artwork and mechanical. You may also want to obtain your management's approval of the mechanical and artwork.

6. *Engraving.* Once you have approved the artwork and mechanical, the agency will release the advertisement for engraving. In addition to being costly, the process is also time-consuming. Without overtime, a four-color offset engraving takes 8 working days; a four-color roto engraving takes 10 to 15 working days. Black-and-white advertisements can be engraved overnight.

7. *Proofs.* A proof is the printed advertisement as it will appear in the magazine. You will be shown a proof for each printing process you have used, usually on the publication's paper stock so you can see exactly how it will appear. You should be aware that four-color proofs are actually the compilation of four separate engraving plates—one each for red, yellow, blue, and black—printed precisely on top of each other. Proofs are pulled for each color as well as the complete color proof you see. Some minor changes can be made after an advertisement has been engraved. Details can be sharpened, color can be toned down or brightened, but if you have any major problems with the proof, you might have to reengrave. It is important when reviewing a proof to understand that the artwork cannot be perfectly reproduced. Mass reproduction has its limitations. The goal is to approach as closely as possible the clarity, intensity, and detail of the artwork. Once you have approved the proof, your advertisement will be released to the magazines.

NEWSPAPER PRODUCTION

Although the steps involved in the production of a newspaper advertisement are the same as those of a magazine advertisement, the entire process is usually much simpler and faster because newspaper advertisements are usually black-and-white. Newspaper production grows complicated only when many different-sized ads must be produced and shipped to a large number of newspapers. You may have noticed that newspaper sizes vary greatly. While some newspapers are endeavoring to standardize their advertising spaces, the process is not yet complete. Your agency traffic person will determine the size that can fit into the most number of papers; however, you may still need to produce two or even three sets of original mechanicals and engravings.

Because newspaper media plans often include papers in many cities, the cost of duplicate materials and shipping or sending materials by sattelite is a larger proportion of newspaper production costs than it is of magazine production costs. Again, time equals money. It's far less expensive to mail materials to newspapers than it is to send them by carrier service at the last minute.

Because of the screen (dots per inch) used in newspaper printing, newspaper reproduction of photography and illustration is inferior to that of magazines. Your creative team should be aware of the limitations of newspaper reproduction and create the advertisement, particularly the artwork, accordingly. Your approval is required of the artwork and mechanical before the advertisement is engraved, and of the proof before it is released to the newspapers.

chapter 13

A personal contract for collaborators

Twelve chapters later—many months, in reality—you have completed the creative process and have a finished print advertisement ready to release to the publications, or a commercial ready to ship to the television stations. Ideally, you will like your advertising, because that proof or thirty seconds of videotape is all you have to show for the months of work, the discussions, arguments, selling, and decisions. If you don't like the advertising, if you don't think it will do the job, surely you can reconstruct what went wrong in the collaborative process, who was to blame, but the reasons why don't seem relevant now. All that matters is that the advertising isn't as good as it should be.

This is an important lesson to learn, and learn over and over again. When all is said and done, this is all that matters: *How good is the advertising?* No excuses.

This book was written to show you how best to work with your agency so that at the moment of truth, when you see your finished advertising, you will be proud of it. If you follow the guidelines, work with talented agency people in a collaborative relationship, sell the advertising through your management so that it emerges stronger rather than diluted, you should have, at the very least, good solid advertising that effectively sells your product or service. However, you have also read about attitudes and actions that poison the advertiser-agency collaboration, that make personal goals the primary priority, and that ultimately weaken the advertising product. Unfortunately, these attitudes and actions all too frequently replace collaboration in the advertiser-agency relationship, but they need not, if everyone in the relationship is committed to collaborating.

You can ensure that commitment and ultimately the best

advertising from your agency if, at the beginning of your relationship with the agency, you propose a personal verbal contract among you, your agency account group and your agency creative team.

THE PERSONAL CONTRACT: WHAT CLIENT AND AGENCY HAVE A RIGHT TO EXPECT FROM EACH OTHER

As discussed in Chapter 2, advertiser and agency companies sign contracts that clearly define job responsibilities, methods of compensation, and other legal matters. However, advertising isn't created by the two companies. It is created by the people involved and the relationship they form with each other. The better the relationship, the more collaborative in nature, the better the advertising that will grow out of it. Therefore, we propose a contract among the people involved in the advertiser-agency relationship. As in any relationship where the parties are involved with each other for long periods of time, there are expectations and commitments, either implicit or explicit. To keep yourself and the agency working within a collaborative relationship, to meet mutual expectations, you and the agency should formally agree to a series of commitments.

THE SEVEN ADVERTISER COMMITMENTS: WHAT YOUR AGENCY EXPECTS FROM YOU

1. A commitment to your agency's best work. Set the goal of great advertising, then do everything you can to help your agency achieve it.

2. Clear, consistent direction. Be an expert on your business. Think through the assignment before calling your agency. Know all the facts before you brief them. Know what you want them to do, when, and why.

> A good client has to be quite directive and tell the agency what's important to him.
>
> *A general manager, food*

[What is a good client?] I'm tempted to cite a number of clients who had implicit faith in me and who bought virtually everything I sold because I wouldn't sell them anything that wasn't right for them. But that's not really necessarily a good client . . . A good client is somebody that has a point of view also, and who sometimes makes sparks. He doesn't always agree but he always makes sense.

Bernard Rosner, Vice President, Creative Director,
Ogilvy & Mather Partners

3. Importance to your business. Any advertiser can ask an agency to help sell her product by creating great advertising. A good advertiser asks the agency to help sell her product *period*. She knows that any problem that affects the sale of her product affects the agency, so she seeks out the agency's opinions in all areas and makes them know that they are an important part of the business.

Good clients ask for more than storyboards. They ask for opinions on important business decisions.

A general manager, food

The best clients . . . make people who are responsible for creative development feel responsible and part of the process.

Richard Rosenbloom, Vice President, Advertising, Card Division,
American Express

4. Open-mindedness and willingness to take a risk. If you want great advertising from your agency, be prepared for new ways of thinking that may make you feel uncomfortable at first. If you want only the obvious, you will get the obvious. If you insist that the agency only do things your way, you will be a "bad client" and will be setting the stage for less-effective advertising.

A good client is one who trusts the agency—who's open to ideas.

J. Leonard Hultgren, founding partner, Scali, McCabe, Sloves

"It's my money and you'll do it my way". . . that's not a client; that's a bully.

Bernard Rosner, Vice President, Creative Director,
Ogilvy & Mather Partners

The best client I ever worked with told me: "Don't show me anything but your choice. I never want to see any alternatives. I don't want to do your job for you."

Herman Davis, Executive Vice President and
Creative Director, Cadwell Davis Partners

The worst . . . took the client-agency relationship to task to the point of establishing an adversarial and very hard-line posture . . . even saying, "I want it done when I want it, how I want it, and I want it done that way," to the point of dictating the kind of advertising he wants to see created and presented at meetings. . . . Then you don't have any mutual respect anymore. All you have is a boss-subordinate role.

Ronald Leong, Group Product Manager, Bristol-Myers

The fact that he would take a risk . . . it's just so beautiful to see someone listen so intently, know what he wanted to do. He didn't do it without reservations. It wasn't like he didn't have to think about it . . . but listen and ask the right questions and finally take the risk. And, by the way, it paid off handsomely.

Bob Neuman, Senior Vice President, Associate
Creative Director, Backer & Spielvogel

5. Focus on the big idea. Never forget what your advertising is trying to do: create an image, a positioning for your product or service, and present it in such a way that consumers will be compelled to buy it. If a big idea isn't in your advertising, no amount of nit-picking can put it there. If it is, most details will take care of themselves.

The colleague I most admire . . . always tried to look for the big idea. He limited his comments to that. He didn't bother about details: He left that to others.

Victor Elkind, Manager of Development,
Main Meal Division, General Foods

My best client was innovative, open to new ideas—he pushed the agency to be more innovative. He asked for more—sent us back to the drawing boards. Creative people liked him. He was open to big ideas. He knew a big idea when he saw one. He never nit-picked.

Susan Hudson, Vice President, Account
Supervisor, Ogilvy & Mather

The best clients have a broad perspective and they are never the people who are second-guessing their bosses. They're people who are genuinely visionary.

Malcolm End, Senior Vice President, Creative
Director, Ogilvy & Mather

6. Support your agency. If you believe that you and the agency have created good advertising, fight for it. You will earn your agency's devotion.

7. Know your advertising ABC's. Take time to learn the fundamentals of advertising. Read a book. Take a course. You'll feel far less dependent on the agency, your advertising judgment will improve, you'll be able to contribute more, you'll be a more effective collaborator, and you will have a great deal more satisfaction.

THE SIX AGENCY COMMITMENTS: WHAT YOU SHOULD EXPECT FROM YOUR AGENCY

1. Commitment to the success of your business. The best agency people are 100 percent committed to the same goal you are: success in the marketplace. Their commitment is evidenced by their time, enthusiasm, work, and knowledge that if you succeed, they succeed.

> [The best agency account person] made suggestions. Not only would she have things to me when they were due and not only would she think to get things done that I didn't ask . . . she'd also come up with suggestions. If I asked her to do something, she'd say "fine," but then she'd come up with something better or take something one or two steps further.
>
> *Ellen Elias, Group Product Manager, Lever Brothers*

> Anybody that's good would want your undivided attention, twenty-four hours a day, seven days a week. They want you to work on their business all the time and to be thinking about their business all the time. . . . They want your blood.
>
> *Bernard Rosner, Vice President, Creative*
> *Director, Ogilvy & Mather Partners*

2. Knowledge of your business. Agency people, particularly the account group, cannot solve your advertising problems unless they have understood and evaluated the market in which you compete. You can help by providing information, but they must do the digging.

3. Open-mindedness. Good agency people are committed to the importance of a good idea, *no matter what its source.* The "not invented here" syndrome has no place in a collaborative relationship.

4. Honesty.

5. Leadership from your account people. Account people are your primary contact and your source of communication within the agency. You have a right to expect that once you and your account person have reached agreement on the direction of work, the account person will effectively convey the decision to the rest of the agency.

> [The best account person] is a wonderful, open person. She related beautifully to clients and creative people. She could galvanize people behind her . . . she had the ability to translate what the client wanted to creative people in such a way that not only did they understand her, but because they respected her and liked her, they *did* it. . . . She made people feel comfortable.
>
> *Mary Seggerman, Senior Product Manager, General Foods*

6. Respect for your position as advertiser. Agency people should know and acknowledge that when all the tugging and arguing and selling are done, they are advertising your product with your money, and the final decisions are your responsibility.

If you can speak openly and honestly with your agency—create a verbal contract by committing to what they can expect from you and what you want to expect from them—and if you can live up to this verbal contract by working within a collaborative relationship, then you *will* get the best advertising from your agency.

Clients get what they deserve, and if they deserve good, enthusiastic, talented agency people, they'll get them; if they deserve boring plodders, they'll get them too. Whatever they want, they'll get.

A general manager, food

You are the person who ultimately creates great advertising.

Case Histories
Analysis and Solutions

The Disrespected Product Manager

ANALYSIS: Having limited authority over the agency places any lower- or middle-level manager in a difficult area known as "influence management." The agency doesn't report to you; you can only influence what they do.

However, this influence-management situation is even more difficult for you. You are suffering from an identity often called the "short pants syndrome," which means that once people have known you as a child, they find it hard to accord you the status of an adult. You worked with the agency when you were an assistant product manager, but even though you now have the responsibilities of a product manager, the agency still perceives you as an assistant.

Your situation may be complicated even further by a few factors. First, you probably haven't proven yourself—either to you or your boss. You may trust your brains, common sense, and knowledge of the product, but because you lack experience, you do not radiate a feeling of confidence. Perceiving this, your boss does not completely trust you and is overly involved in your work. Second, the agency is comfortable working with your boss, and they can obtain approvals faster and with less hassle by going over your head. Finally, the agency may be testing you— seeing how far they can go before you force them to deal with you.

SOLUTION: If you can establish your influence with the agency, you will automatically establish it with your boss. Therefore, your first step is to tell the account executive *and the account supervisor* that you want to meet with them. Reaching up a level to include the account supervisor is a bold step that is a statement of your position as "The Client" of a service company. The account supervisor may be reluctant at first to meet with you (to meet may be a threat to his status), but he will comply because you, the client, have requested the meeting.

At the meeting, tell the account executive and the account supervisor that you will be the primary agency contact from now on, and that you need and want their help to make your business and you a success. Tell them that they have the experience you lack at the moment and you value their suggestions. Then propose a verbal contract with them such as that described in Chapter 13. In this one meeting, you will have established your influence, involved the agency in your business so that your goals become their goals, and committed your support to the agency. In sum, you have established a collaborative relationship and created an environment that leads to getting the best advertising from your agency.

After you have met with the agency, meet with your boss and inform her of the agreement you have reached with the agency. Reassure her that you will make her aware of the status of all major projects and will involve her in major decisions; then ask her to support you by referring the agency to you if they continue to look to her for approval. By asserting yourself with the agency and informing your boss of your action, you will have both established your influence and reconfirmed the abilities that led your boss to promote you in the first place.

CASE 2.

The Disrespected Account Executive

ANALYSIS: Your account executive's inability to gain respect can cause major problems for you. Your copy could be off strategy; creative and media people may be devoting less time and enthusiasm to your business; closing dates and air dates could be missed. Day-to-day work would be easier for you and your advertising might be better if the agency assigned a stronger account executive. On the other hand, the account executive has every right to gain experience, to feel his way with his support groups and experiment with management methods. Unfortunately, his experience may be gained at your expense.

SOLUTION: Postpone asking for the account executive's removal. Unless a major problem has arisen on your business since the account executive was assigned, the agency will want you to give him an opportunity to succeed. However, you can cover yourself by making certain that his boss, the account supervisor, is aware of your direction for all major projects. Temporarily put all direction to the agency in writing, with copies to the account supervisor. Written direction is more time-consuming, but it is one way you can be certain your direction and expectations are communicated.

You can also help yourself by helping your account executive gain the respect of his creative and media people. Simply show your respect for him in meetings. Whenever possible, support what he says. If you are respected within the agency, your respect for the account executive will immediately be adopted by the support groups. As he gains experience, he will not only be more effective on your business, he will also be personally committed to you because of the help you gave him.

CASE 3.

About-Face!

ANALYSIS: Most agencies would jump at the chance to proceed to production with a campaign about which they are excited. Therefore, there must be something—or more likely some*one*—that changed their mind. In all likelihood, your account and creative teams did not clear the new campaigns with a key senior person before they presented them to you. This senior person, either the creative director or the management supervisor, must have serious misgivings about the potential effectiveness of the campaign.

SOLUTION: Your first task is to find out who at the agency doesn't like the campaign and why. If possible, arrange a face-to-face meeting with that person to learn his point of view and to explain yours. If you are compensating the agency on a commission or flat-fee basis, by all means let the agency proceed with new copy even before your meeting. It will cost you only the fee for drawing the storyboards. If you are on a cost-plus compensation system, you ought to have the meeting with the key person before you spend more money on copy development.

However, you need to focus on the agency's reasons for changing their mind, and they need to hear yours. If accord cannot be reached during your discussions, use testing to help in your collective decision.

This unfortunate situation can happen at a large agency when advertising must be approved through senior people who are several layers above the people actually doing the work. Their approval process can add a week or so to the already-lengthy advertising-development process. However, all accounts should have the attention of senior agency creative and account people. These people didn't get to the top for nothing.

Your account people should not have presented copy until all at the agency had seen it. They are clearly at fault here. However, the most important thing is the quality of the advertising on which you are going to spend your media budget. If you consistently focus on that, inconveniences, even major ones, will fall into perspective.

CASE 4.

The Dictator

ANALYSIS: Even though the product manager is happy with the advertisement she created, her actions are a serious threat to the work your agency is trying to do for her business, and a serious threat to your career. Although the ad has not been tested, the most experienced people at your agency believe that it is unlikely to produce marketplace results. Eventually, your client and her management will become unhappy with the advertising and the agency.

As a management supervisor, you are being evaluated on the success of your client's business as well as on the advertising you create for her. That's why you have tried so hard to obtain her superior's help to teach the product manager how to work with the agency.

SOLUTION: Unfortunately, there may not be a solution to this case. In real life, the product manager continued to write her own advertising; she got her own ideas and nothing more.

What could have been tried, but wasn't, was an informal meeting between the account executive, the original senior creative team, and the product manager. At the meeting, the creative people could have shown her all their advertising for other clients that had worked in the marketplace. They could have asked her to allow them to try to create that type of advertising for her . . . at the same time reassuring her that they would execute her ideas as faithfully as possible. It could have been arranged, budget permitting, that her ads always be tested against theirs. This is expensive and time-consuming, but where the priority is to create the best advertising, it may be a necessary step.

On the other hand, a meeting such as this, no matter how informal, can still be a confrontation. With a frightened person, such as the product manager, it could have backfired.

CASE 5.

Possessiveness

ANALYSIS AND SOLUTION: Of course, you are free to make any request that you like, but your agency will probably not accede. This would be to your benefit.

Think for a moment about the creative process. A team

learns the facts behind an advertising problem. Then they need time to digest those facts, to sort them out in various ways (often in the subconscious, some psychologists believe). This digestion and sorting often happens best when the creative team is busy solving another advertiser's problems. At some point, usually a few days later, the team is ready to actively work on your problems.

Because they have had a chance to take their minds off your business, they are able to approach the new challenge with more objectivity and a fresh thinking. If they only worked on your account, they could lose the important perspective of your target, present advertising too much in your point of view instead of your potential customers'. The chances of your continuing to obtain great work from the best team on the business are enhanced because they work on other accounts as well as yours.

CASE 6.

The Complacent Copy Contact

ANALYSIS: You are in trouble! Your client has threatened to remove his business from the agency and you must bring the situation to the attention of the president. You must prepare a succinct review of the facts as you see them and propose a solution.

SOLUTION: In this true case, there were two factors contributing to the increased tensions. First, the advertising director was reporting to a new president of his company. He had worked with the previous president for many years and was, therefore, under new pressures to prove himself. The copy contact understood the pressures facing the advertising director, but mistakenly attributed all of the problems in the relationship to him.

Second, without being conscious of the fact, the copy contact had started to take her position and her client for granted. She wrote and presented work that was good enough, but not outstanding. Since she did not have to present the advertising to her busy president, no one at the agency was aware that her work and her attitude were slipping. She began to feel that the account belonged to her, not to the agency.

When she met with the president, he did not wait to hear her solution to the problem, but instead immediately suggested that he, the copy contact, and the advertising director have lunch together. It took place a few weeks later at the president's private luncheon club. Everyone was nervous except the president, who made small talk through cocktails and through the appetizer. He finally brought up the relationship problem by asking the copy contact how long she had worked on the advertising director's account. When she responded that it was about five years, the president made a brilliant move. He turned to the advertising director and said, "Molly's been on your business for a long time. What do you say about making a change?" The president offered to fire the copy contact off the account in front of her client! The advertising director, horrified, said that he didn't want to lose the copy contact.

Why was the president's move so brilliant? He told the advertising director that his business was very important to the agency and proved it by offering to replace the copy contact. He told the copy contact that she was expendable, thereby snapping her out of her complacency. Also, his gamble that the relationship was basically good paid off when the advertising director immediately said he wanted the copy contact to remain on the business.

After lunch the advertising director and copy contact had the talk that should have taken place six months earlier. They realized how the tension and complacency had occurred. With their new understanding, they were able to collaborate on the advertising challenges set forth by the client company's new president.

CASE 7.

The Correct and Only Priority

ANALYSIS AND SOLUTION: If your agency truly believes that business results should not influence advertising decisions, then you probably need a new agency. Chances are, however, that it is your account executive who doesn't understand her job or the advertising business.

Your agency does have a right to look at your analysis for the causes of the business decline and try to determine the role of the advertising. You certainly owe it to your business not to stop running effective copy if the problem lies elsewhere.

However, business results are the only priority here, and a serious decline should command total agency concern and action. You need to do two things. First, let the account executive know in no uncertain terms exactly what you expect of her: total commitment to the success of your business. Second, escalate the problem so that your senior management contacts agency senior management. You need immediate analysis of the problem from their perspective and, if warranted, new advertising.

If the agency, particularly the account group, had been properly involved in your business to begin with, it is they who should have come to you with a proposal for exploring new advertising directions. It is just the types of attitude in this case that can poison the productive advertiser-agency relationship.

CASE 8.

Twenty Questions

ANALYSIS AND SOLUTION: While it is certainly frustrating to have to return to your technical or product people time and time again, you must remember that even the tiniest fact can form the basis of a campaign, or help a creative team humanize a product for your target market.

You may have to chase down a lot of answers that are never used, but when they are used, they can be very important. For example, the small size of a video cassette player was communicated more effectively when engineers confirmed that it was about one fourth the size of most VCR's. A commercial for a new floor-cleaning product was written based on the fact that many women don't wear shoes around the house.

Unfortunately, questions often occur to the creative people, not at the formal briefing but later, when they have explored the information more deeply.

Timing Is Everything

ANALYSIS AND SOLUTION: Although it may seem strange at first—and it certainly could take more time—it is best to wait to present your advertising idea until after the agency has made its first presentation to you.

There are two reasons. First, being given the full responsibility to solve a problem is motivating and exciting. Your creative and account people will be far more committed to developing outstanding campaigns if they know that you are looking to them to be the heroes, and if they don't have to compete with you to come up with a campaign that you must ultimately approve.

Imagine the drop in your own motivation if your boss asked you to write the first draft of a marketing plan and then told you what he would do if he were writing it. In essence, he'd be doing a major part of the job he'd just asked you to do. You'd be understandably demoralized, and, if time were a problem, you might just do things his way instead of contributing your own ideas.

Second, if you give your agency your ideas at the start of a creative exploratory, you are asking them to agree or disagree with you before they have a chance to start thinking about the advertising. Even if you have limited authority, you are still their client; they want you to like their work.

Not giving your ideas at the start of an assignment doesn't mean that you shouldn't give them at all. Many outstanding campaigns grew from advertisers' ideas. The question is not *if* but *when*. To best motivate your agency, to get the best advertising from them, delegate the full task and responsibility to them.

Then, after the copy is presented, if you don't like their ideas better than yours, ask them to execute your idea as part of the revision process.

CASE 10.

The Self-Fulfilling Prophecy

ANALYSIS: This case is an excellent example of an advertiser-agency relationship that started off on the wrong foot—and got progressively worse. Eventually, trust and open communication were totally lacking. Both advertiser and agency did a lot of things wrong. About the only thing they did right somehow was to develop a winning campaign.

Although the advertiser did show cost concern by always driving into the city, keeping costs down rather than developing outstanding advertising was the major focus of the relationship. The advertiser's position is understandable because of their previous experience, but, nevertheless, they went into the relationship assuming they could not trust the agency.

On a very tight budget, this advertiser should have contracted a fixed-fee compensation system with the agency. That way, the agency would have been paid a fixed amount of money every month and the advertiser would not have had to keep track of the amount of time the agency spent on the business. That would have been the agency's concern.

The advertiser was naive in asking for only three storyboards. While it may have cost more to draw additional boards for presentation, the bulk of the cost of a creative exploratory is in the development stage when the creative people think of the ideas. Usually, after they have explored many different executions, the agency will look at all the commercials and see how many are worthy of being drawn for presentation.

The agency was also naive to have thought that the advertiser would be overjoyed at seeing more work than was asked for, especially as a surprise. They did not demonstrate cost concern to their clients.

SOLUTION: Talk. Communicate. Discuss mutual expectations (see Chapter 13) and decide how best to work together in the future. Bringing everything out in the open—plus changing the agency compensation system—could help to make this a productive working relationship.

In actuality, however, the advertiser and agency never did talk about how they were working together. They terminated the relationship less than a year after the agency was first hired.

CASE 11.

Cancellation

ANALYSIS: As an account supervisor, you are in a no-win situation. If you cancel the creative presentation, you incur the displeasure of both your client and your creative people. You also risk missing the magazine closing dates. If you present the advertisement as planned, your client will perceive the same problems you do and will send the agency back to make revisions. You, of course, will look foolish for not having noticed that strategic elements were missing, and, worst of all, you will be in a position of trying to convince your client to run copy that you know isn't yet correct. All that is to be gained from holding the meeting is your avoidance of an unpleasant situation and the possible agreement of your client as to the basic direction of the advertisement.

WHAT SHOULD HAVE HAPPENED: Without question the account supervisor should have cancelled the meeting. If he was collaborating with his client, he would have kept his focus on producing the best advertising and would have had the honesty and strength to deal with both his client's and the creative people's frustration. In the final analysis, all that matters is the quality of the advertisement. The memory of a late presentation can fade, but the advertisement remains forever part of the history of the product or service.

WHAT ACTUALLY HAPPENED: The account supervisor did not cancel the meeting. The off-strategy copy was presented and was badly received. In fact, the advertiser's generally good opinion of the agency was seriously, though only temporarily, jeopardized. The account supervisor salvaged his position only by defending the good basic direction of the advertisement. The only benefit from the meeting was that the creative people felt they had had their opportunity to present their first choice. They never realized that they hurt their credibility in the process. After six revisions, the advertisement was finally approved. It was tested and scored at the "average" level.

CASE 12.

It Comes When It Comes

ANALYSIS: It is utter nonsense to believe that "creative comes when it comes." It comes when the art director and copywriter go looking for it. Creating advertising involves discipline as well as talent, and a timetable is a catalyst that gets a job started.

You cannot give your agency too little time to develop advertising; nor can you give them too much. Too little time could mean that you get only their first idea, which is not necessarily their best. Too much time can mean that the agency postpones thinking about a project. To creative people who are initially afraid to attack a problem, the fear grows. (Surprisingly, many creative people are unsure of their abilities and don't relax until they are well into a problem.)

Allow your agency two to three weeks to develop advertising—a week or two more if they ask for it. If the agency needs a few extra days at the end, give it to them if you can. They may have reviewed what they have already created and want to explore additional directions. Try to build a buffer into your timetable.

When reasonable, most timetables are a stimulus, not a hindrance.

SOLUTION: If you cannot help your assistant account executive understand the above, write her a letter and send a copy to her boss. As the assistant learns more about the advertising business, she should see where she is wrong.

CASE 13.

The Stubborn Agency

ANALYSIS: Even in the best of collaborative relationships, advertiser and agency can reach an impasse where each believes his solution to an advertising problem is totally correct. In this case, the agency did not present an alternate visual not because they were stubborn, but because they could not create an alternate visual that they believed was as strong as the original. They could have prepared a weak alternative just to prove the strength of the original; however, that would have been dishonest. More importantly, any time an agency presents an advertisement, they must be prepared to run it. No agency wants to be forced to run their "straw dog." On the other hand, as the advertiser, you have every right to see an alternate visual that both solves your problems and is the agency's best effort.

SOLUTIONS: There is no one correct solution to this advertising impasse; however, two of those explained below do require that the agency prepare an alternate visual. No matter how strongly the agency believes in its position, you are the advertiser and, therefore, have the right to see alternate advertising and even to choose to run what could be a weaker advertisement, if it solves your problem.

The first solution is to ask the agency to create a new visual and then test both your and the agency's preferred advertisements. One relatively inexpensive way of testing a newspaper advertisement is to conduct a split-run test in the newspaper itself. Many papers are equipped to split their circulations into two matched samples and deliver a different advertisement to each sample. If the agency includes an offer for free information in the body copy of both versions of the advertisement, the strength of each version can be measured by the number of requests for information it elicits. The version with the larger number of requests is the winner. Another relatively inexpensive way of testing is to obtain a communications measurement of the major product or service benefits.

The second solution is to ask the agency to prepare an alternate visual and use judgment. It is possible they may like it better than the original; however, should you alone prefer the new visual, you can choose to run it. Your risk is that it may be weaker. Do not worry that your collaborative relationship will be jeopardized. Unless your insistence on doing things your way becomes a habit and you cease to work in a collaborative relationship, the agency will gracefully accept defeat and move on.

The third solution is simply to run the agency's recommended advertisement. Trust their expertise and view their hesitancy to prepare an alternate visual as proof of the strength of their convictions. What is your risk? It is the same as in the second solution: The advertisement you run may be weaker than it should be.

CASE 14.

The First Copy Review

ANALYSIS: While this unusual copy meeting may seem intimidating at first, you are actually in a no-lose situation that presents a major opportunity for you to impress both your management and the agency. Both are aware of your lack of advertising and product experience and expect only a few intelligent comments from you. However, should you be able to contribute significantly to the advertising, you will simultaneously impress your management and tell the agency that even though you are a new assistant product manager, you have your management's respect and the agency must work with you.

SOLUTION: The assistant product manager in this true case was extremely successful, mainly by using his common sense. Prior to the big meeting, he reviewed all the advertising that had been written for his product. He reviewed all the call reports to learn how the advertising had been received, and he reviewed all test results of advertising that had been approved and produced. He also reviewed competitive advertising and, of course, the strategy to which the new copy was being executed. His purpose was to determine his own point of view on what he wanted the new copy to communicate—what he planned to look for as the copy was being presented. Once he reached a point of view, he discussed it with his group product manager both to learn whether his thinking was on target and to gain some measure of psychological support before the meeting.

At the meeting, the agency presented three commercials and recommended them all for rough production and testing. The assistant product manager was, of course, called upon first. His initial comments applauded the positive aspect of the presentation—in this case, a wide range of executions. He then commented on each execution, focusing on the idea inherent in each rather than on individual copy lines or visual situations. The first commercial presented used the food-imitation product as a snack rather than as a main-course food. The assistant product manager questioned whether he wanted the product used as a snack, because snack use would result in lower volume than if the food substitute was served during a meal. The second commercial included humor, but it did not make the assistant laugh. He said so, but admitted that his response was a personal reaction. The final commercial emphasized the product's imitation qualities by using look-alike celebrities. The assistant felt that the execution emphasized the differences rather than the similarities between the imitation and its real counterpart.

The assistant product manager's review of the advertising was excellent because his comments were given in the true spirit of collaboration. He was sensitive to the agency and the vast amount of work they had created. He reacted as a person and trusted his reactions. He confined his comments to the big idea rather than nitpicking the words or visuals. He stated his problems, not the solutions. In short, in one meeting, he proved his copy judgment to himself, his management, and the agency—and he contributed ways to improve the advertising.

This is another example of how you are the person who ultimately creates great advertising.

Appendix

The 1987 *Salz Survey of Advertiser-Agency Relations*

In early April 1987, questionnaires were mailed to 201 senior advertising or marketing executives at 186 of the top 200 advertiser companies and subsidiaries as ranked by Leading National Advertisers. Questionnaires were also sent to the president or CEO at the top 100 agencies as ranked by *Advertising Age*.

Fourteen advertisers were not contacted because they were state or local governments, associations that could not measure sales results, did not work with an outside advertising agency, or had declined to participate in the survey the previous year.

Responses were received from 33 percent of the advertisers and 43 percent of the agencies. These response rates are considered good for senior executives. The questionnaires and, therefore, the responses were anonymous.

CONCLUSIONS

1. There is a major opportunity for top advertisers to take action—specific action—to improve the productivity of their agency relationships and, therefore, the quality of the advertising they are getting from their agencies. In a competitive marketplace, those advertisers who take this action could see a significant increase in sales.
   - Only slightly more than one out of two advertisers is currently getting the best advertising from its agencies.
     —Top agencies reported that they are able to do their best work for only 59 percent of their major clients. (This is a three-percentage-point improvement over 1986.)
   - Top advertisers are only barely satisfied with the advertising they are getting from their agencies. Their rating was even lower in 1987 than it was in 1986.
     —Advertisers rated the quality of the advertising their

189

agencies develop with a mean of 7.1 on a 1 to 10 scale this year compared to last year's 7.5.

- However, advertisers could see a large increase in sales and profits if they were able to obtain their agencies' best advertising more frequently.
  —If their agencies produced their best work all the time, top advertisers estimated a 24 percent increase in sales and a 23 percent increase in profits.

2. According to top advertisers and agencies, the greatest opportunity for action to improve the productivity of the advertiser-agency relationship and, therefore, the quality of advertising, is in five areas:

- *The management skills* of the people involved in advertising development—both advertiser and agency people.
  —Advertisers felt that only 63 percent of their own people who manage the day-to-day relationship are good at working with the agency. Agency people felt that only 49 percent of those people are good.
  —Although the skills of all the contributors to the collaboration that is the advertiser-agency relationship are obviously crucial, advertisers and agencies each believe that the skills of the other in developing advertising is more important than their own skills.
- *The standards advertisers set* for their agencies' work— their desire for outstanding advertising and receptivity to new ideas.
  —Advertisers increased their rating in importance of being open to new ideas dramatically in 1987. (Fifty-one percent rated "Very Important" versus 39 percent in 1986.)
- *Agency people liking to work on the business.*
- *Good communication* at all levels between advertisers and agencies.
- *A limited number of advertiser-approval levels.*

3. Obtaining the best work from an advertising agency has far less to do with money than with the preceding factors.

- Both top advertisers and top agencies ranked agency profit and size of an advertising budget far below other factors in importance as reasons for obtaining or developing high-quality advertising.

TABLE 1
Advertisers

Q. On a scale of 1–10, 10 being the best possible, how would you rate the advertising you get from each of your agency(ies)?

Base: Total Agency(ies) Rated	Ratings of Advertising (154 = 100 percent)
	Percent
1	1
2	–
3	1
4	3
5	7
6	21
7	21
8	32
9	12
10	3
Mean rating:	7.1%

TABLE 2
Advertisers

Q. For those agency(ies) you rated highly, please indicate how important each of the following reasons is for your high ratings.

Base: Total Advertisers	Rated 5 *"Very Important"* Scale 1–5 (67 = 100 percent)
	Percent
We truly want outstanding advertising.	70
There are good agency people on our business.	61
We're open to new advertising ideas.	51
Agency people like to work on our business.	49
We don't have too many approval levels for advertising.	31
Our product managers/group product managers/advertising managers are good at working with the agency.	28
We have good communication at all levels with our agency(ies).	27
Our senior management is good at managing the agency.	18
Our business(es) are in high-interest categories.	16
The agency makes what they consider to be a fair profit on our business.	15
We have a large advertising budget.	12

TABLE 3
Advertisers

Q. What percentage of your product managers/advertising managers—or those people who are in day-to-day contact with your agency(ies)—are good at working with them?

Base: Total Advertisers	Good at Working with the Agency (67 = 100 Percent)
Percent	*Percent*
100	6
75	48
60	3
50	31
25	9
10	1
DK	1
Mean percentage:	62.6%

TABLE 4
Advertisers

Q. If your agency(ies) did its (their) best work for you 100 percent of the time, what kind of impact would you estimate this would have on your sales?

Base: Total Advertisers	Impact on Sales (67 = 100 Percent)
Percent	*Percent*
+ 100	—
+ 75	1
+ 50	15
+ 25	40
+ 17.5	1
+ 10	27
+ less than 10	4
No answer/can't measure	10
Mean percentage:	24.3%

TABLE 5
Advertisers

Q. If your agency(ies) did its (their) best work for you 100 percent of the time, what kind of impact would you estimate this would have on your profits?

Base: Total Advertisers	Impact on Profits (67 = 100 Percent)
Percent	*Percent*
+ 100	—
+ 75	3
+ 50	9
+ 25	34
+ 15	1
+ 10	30
+ less than 10	4
No answer/can't measure	18
Mean increase in profits predicted:	23.0%

TABLE 6
Agencies

Q. For what percentage of your major clients is your agency able to do its best advertising?

Base: Total Agencies	Percentage of Major Clients (42 = 100 Percent)
Percent	*Percent*
100	—
90	14
80	19
70	5
60	14
50	19
40	12
30	12
20	2
10	2
Mean rating:	58.57%

TABLE 7
Agencies

Q. Please evaluate the importance of the following factors in influencing the quality of the advertising you create for each of your major clients.

Base:	*Rated 5* *"Very Important"* *Scale: 1–5* *(42 = 100 Percent)*
	Percent
The client is open to new ideas in advertising.	76
The client really wants outstanding work.	71
There are a limited number of approval levels for advertising.	67
Agency people like to work on the business.	55
There is good communication at all levels between the client and agency.	52
Product managers/group product managers/ advertising managers are good at working with the agency.	48
Senior client management is good at working with the agency.	48
The agency makes a fair profit on the account.	26
We put our best people on their business.	24
Advertising is a big contributor to their bottom line.	17
The client has a large advertising budget.	5
The client is in a business that agency people find interesting.	2
The client is a major company, important in its field.	–

TABLE 8
Advertisers and Agencies

Q. For those agency(ies) you rated highly, please indicate how important each of the following reasons is for your high ratings.
Q. Please evaluate the importance of the following factors in influencing the quality of the advertising you create for each of your major clients.

| Base: Advertisers | Rated 5—"Very Important" Scale: 1–5 | | Difference |
| | Advertisers (82 = 100 Percent) | Agencies (67 = 100 Percent) | |
	Percent	Percent	Percentage Points
Not too many approval levels for advertising.	31	67	+36
Senior management is good at working with/managing the agency.	18	48	+30
Good communication at all levels between client and agency.	27	52	+25
Open to new advertising ideas.	51	76	+25
Product managers/group product managers/advertising managers are good at working with the agency.	28	48	+20
The agency makes what they consider to be a fair profit on our business.	15	26	+11
Agency people like to work on our/the business.	49	55	+ 6
We truly want outstanding advertising.	70	71	+ 1
We/client have/has a large advertising budget.	12	5	– 7
Client business is interesting to agency people.	16	2	–14
There are good agency people/we put our best people on our/the business.	61	24	–37

TABLE 9
Agencies

Q. At your major client companies, what percentage of the people with whom your agency has day-to-day contact are good at working with the agency?

Base: Total Agencies	*Percentage of People Good at Working With Agency (42 = 100 Percent)*
Percent	*Percent*
100	–
75	31
50	36
25	29
10	5
Mean percentage:	48.69%

Index

A

ABC, 129
Abrahamsen, Ray, 58
Account executive, 21
Account management, 32–34
  marketing services, 14–15
Account manager, 33–34
Account supervisor, 20, 21, 42
Advertiser-Agency Relations, Salz
  Survey of, 189–197
Advertising
  approval process, 127–141
  effective, 3
  great, definition of 2–5, 30
  importance of, 2
  judging, 105–125
  money spent on, 2
  objectives of, 2–3
  preselling, 135
  reviewing, 105–125
  specialized, 16
Advertising Age, 130
Advertising agency
  assignments, 80–84
  briefing the, 93–101
  commitments, 171–173
  compensation, 24–25
  definition of an, 14
  delegation to, 58–59
  evaluation of, 87–99
  first meeting with, 75–76
  giving information to, 60–61
  involvement in your business, 71–73
  learning about, 73–74
  management, *see* Management

organization, 13–29
profits, 25–26
responsibility of, 79–80
services, 14–24
size of, 26–28
as source of great advertising,
  5
Advertising manager, 7
Agency producer, 156
Alcohol, Tobacco & Firearms,
  Bureau of, 128
American Association of Advertis-
  ing Agencies (AAAA), 14, 15,
  16, 132
American Express
  Card Division of, 11, 45, 69, 118,
    169
  Industry Marketing Division of,
    48, 74, 98, 120, 121, 125
Animatic production, 145
Appreciation, showing, 62–63,
  123
Approval of advertising
  legal and regulatory, 127–131
  management, 131–137
Art director, 19
Art supervisor, 19
Assignment, agency, 80–84
  continuing, 82–84
Association of National Advertisers
  (ANA), 1, 3, 12, 56, 132
Atlas, Jeff, 36, 52, 100, 120
Attitudes, disruptive, 48–55
Auditing Productivity (Weilbacher),
  47, 56, 80, 92, 132, 141
Auditions, 146, 152
Authority, relaxation of, 46–47

199